JUST PLAIN PEOPLE

JUST

Tales and Truths

B. Csatory 14

PLAIN PEOPLE
of Amish Life

E. R. Beachy

STACKPOLE
BOOKS

Published by
STACKPOLE BOOKS
Cameron and Kelker Streets
P.O. Box 1831
Harrisburg, PA 17105

Printed in the United States of America

Originally published as *TALES FROM THE PEOLI ROAD: Wit and humor of very real people, who just happen to be Amish*

Illustrations by Bill Csatary
Cover design by Tracy Patterson

First Edition

10 9 8 7 6 5 4 3 2 1

Library of Congress Cataloging-in-Publication Data

Beachy, Eli R., 1950–
    Just plain people : tales and truths of Amish life / E.R. Beachy.
    — 2nd ed.
        p.   cm.
    Rev. ed. of: Tales from the Peoli Road. ©1992.
    ISBN 0-8117-3003-4 : $9.95
        1. Amish—Ohio—Social life and customs—anecdotes.
    2. Amish—Ohio—Social life and customs—Humor. I. Beachy,
    Eli R., 1950–   Tales from the Peoli Road.   II. Title.
    F550.M45B4   1993
    977.1'0088287— dc20   92-37477
                                                          CIP

Contents

Preface

It had been a long time since a dose of reality made me feel that bad. That big ox of an Ivan and I had been visiting for near an hour at the Mount Hope horse sale one day. As he went off to the hardware, a friend of mine, city girl she is, came over and in total innocence said, "How can you guys do it?"

"What's that, Kelly?"

"How can you stand and laugh and talk and talk for an hour? What is there to say? We in the city don't do that."

Some would say that Kelly has it all. Nice house, good job, beautiful car, just about everything—and here she was dumbfounded that dumb old us, just being us, could entertain ourselves quite well without spending a dime. She had come to our neck of the woods sort of feeling sorry folks around here don't have the life of convenience she does. I think she was feeling bad that day when she left, making the discovery that money can't buy the peace of mind friendship can. Out of these friendships has come a tradition that's alive and well among the Plain People: storytelling.

To many, Amish society is shrouded in secrecy and veiled in misperception. Beyond the tourist attraction, however, lies a people, a real society of very real people. Not saints, not sinners, the Amish are people doing the best they can the only way they know how in order to get by. They are remarkable folks who just happen to drive to church in a buggy, and they have their share of adventures—and misadventures.

Talking and telling stories have always been part of this life I know so well. There is no television or radio here, only each other. With each other the Amish live the stories of life. Some are amusing, others might bring a tear, but each and every one we learn from. Storytelling is an ancient art, a forgotten treasure to some, and a fact of life in Amish country.

Just Plain People is a collection of some of those stories and is pure fiction, plain and simple. And E. R. Beachy is a pen name. Please remember that and don't you dare let any of us who were actually there when these events took place convince you of something else. Fiction and a pen name, and with that out of the way, may you enjoy.

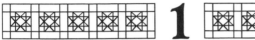 **1**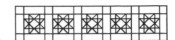

First
there is birth

Some might call it odd that an entire road full of people can live without electricity today. Others might say it's peculiar those same folk can also get by quite well without the automobile. Even more might be struck dumb to learn there are some without the indoor plumbing. When we see that back home, down just about any road through the Peoli Valley, we call it Unser Leit, Our People. When strangers see it, they call it the Amish.

It strikes folks strange down our way that the Amish have become the largest tourist attraction in Ohio these days. Two big, multimillion-dollar amusement parks used to come first and second, but not anymore. Now it's the Plain People. It makes no sense to us, to be honest with you. We've been living our own life our own way without too much help all these years. Now, within the last fifteen years, all sorts of people come running into what Ohio calls Amish country like they're trying to find something.

Maybe it's because they forgot some things more than they're looking to find something new. There's nothing the Amish are doing today that wasn't the way all of rural America was doing things ninety years ago. If those visitors are coming looking for something spiritual, though, they sure have a roundabout way of finding that, too. All they'd have to do is ask, but city people do have a tendency to be a bit strange anyway.

You know I was to Chicago once. I'll tell you, it's as bad as Millersburg on a Saturday these days. People rushing here and there, all seeming to be looking for some sort of excitement. We don't need the big city for the wild times. Around here at least, we all had a wild time five years ago one New Year's Eve.

It was an hour or so before dark when half a dozen of us had congregated down at the mill, holding what we call our New Year's Eve Gala. It was crisp, but not winter-cold yet that year. As a matter of fact, with the exception of substituting my black felt for the summer straw hat, I think I was wearing the exact same clothes I was wearing the beginning of October.

The crowd that had collected likes to consider ourselves the trustees of the Peoli Valley, the wise ones and all, but the womenfolk of the area much prefer to brand us for what we are—the loafers. At any rate, we was all standing there, sipping on a little of the homemade root beer Levi likes to brew up when all of a sudden, running down the road, here comes Noah. He was running so fast I was afraid the house was on fire.

"No, no," he managed to gasp. "It's my wife. The little one is finally on the way!"

We all started grinning, thinking of a new arrival in our community, as we watched the big, burly redhead run over to the phone booth to call Mike, a local fellow who likes to drive

for the Amish. You may have heard that the Plain People don't
go for having a telephone and that's true, but there's nothing
wrong with its proper use. Same with the automobile. Most
wouldn't want to own one but, when need be, around here a
ride can be quite handy. Sure enough, in just a few minutes,
here comes Mike in his old blue Chevy pickup. He and Noah
talk, Noah jumps in and off they go, down Old 23 headed for
County Hospital.

Such a joyous occasion as this long-expected addition to the community called for another round of the root beer. We wasn't but three or four sips into the mug when here comes Mike, racing up the road past us and right on up the North Road. This was confusing, but trust old Mervin to advise patience, and he was right.

Sure enough, in just a few minutes, here comes Mike down the road again. This time he's a-blowing the air horn and hooting and hollering out the window. He was going quick, powerful quick in fact, but not so fast that we couldn't see that Noah was sitting there in the cab of that truck with a feed sack over his head.

It seems that Noah was hoping that we would have dispersed by now or, if not, then we wouldn't recognize him, but that wasn't to be. We all instantly grasped the situation and knew that feed sack wasn't what was so important. What the big thing was all about was between Mike and Noah there in the truck.

It's hard—no, it's outright impossible—to have a son, which turned out to be twin sons, first children born in the county that year, at County Hospital when your wife is sitting on the steps of the home place up the North Road, wondering what's taking you so long to make that phone call.

Sagas like that remind me there are some who believe the Amish don't take to doctoring. That's a silly thought, there being nothing any more precious than human life. The problem comes in when folks realize the Amish are genetically bred to be cheap, closer to a dollar bill than George Washington. Close enough to our money we can make the buffalo on each and every nickel outright groan at times. Of us all, though, there's none as cheap as Old Miller.

Old Miller thought it horrible our doctor hereabouts charged $4.75 for a shot. What Miller did was to stop by one day and had the doc show him how to give injections. It probably cost a lot more to buy them needle things than to get a shot, but you couldn't tell Miller that. Miller left the doc's office happy as a clam, whistling through what teeth he's got left, and filed that information away in his mind.

As fate would have it, it wasn't but a few weeks later that Mrs. Miller got to feeling run down. Old Miller put two and two together. When the calves in the barn get run down, he gives them a shot of vitamin B–6 or something. If it's good for the calves, it's got to be good for the wife. Since he knew how to give human injections, that's what Miller did, and eventually Mrs. Miller pepped right up.

It was between the shot and the eventually that things got pretty interesting, though. First thing was that Mrs. Miller's eyes started to water. Then she swelled up all over. Then she itched and itched every place she could and a few others as well. It finally passed and she felt fine, but there were some tense moments at the Miller household.

Needless to say, a few days later Old Miller happened to be by the doctor's office. Just a hypothetical question, of course, but he wondered what would happen should a man accidentally give his wife an overdose of, let's say, B–6. I think it was B–6, but maybe it was B–14. Might even of been kelp, but that's neither here nor there.

Well, the doc is pretty sharp. First thing he said was, "A man don't think much of his spouse to be doing that," and Miller, he nods. Yep, it was B–6. The doc went on how her eyes would water, she'd swell up and itch, same symptoms but she'd soon be fine. Might take a day, maybe two, but she'd be all right. Just then the doctor threw in a little kicker.

"You know," the doc said, "there's a little-known side effect. Ninety-nine times out of one hundred, the lady in question ends up pregnant in the next thirty days. You already got sixteen of your own, don't you, Miller?"

Miller, he starts gasping for air, nods and goes dashing

out of the office. Now it could be Miller is in that distinct minority, that one percent of lucky people. Could be that the doc was just having some fun, too. However it worked out, some say there was a very ladylike sigh of relief coming from the Miller house a couple of weeks later and the count still stands at sixteen.

Having sixteen offsprings can be more of a handicap than just keeping the cupboard bare. It was a few years back when Miller got the notice that the Internal Revenue Service would like to have a chat with him. Quaking in his shoes like every good individual does in that situation of being about to be audited, Miller got himself a driver and over to the tax man they went.

Come to find out, the notion of Miller having sixteen dependents at the home place didn't sit well with the IRS. What they needed was some proof of this large family. With a nod of his head, Miller was off for home to get exactly what the government wanted.

I'd imagine you can estimate the tax man's surprise when Miller returned but didn't have birth certificates. Why bother with paper when you can present the real thing? All sixteen of them trooping into the office, introducing themselves and shaking hands with the nice man. Miller's not giving anybody any more shots lately, but the IRS is leaving him alone, too.

As a very young man, I had a chance to experience first-hand the benefits of modern medicine myself. Being five, maybe six years of age, I had gotten pretty big for my britches. Being a bighead happens in every faith, believe me. It just seems it takes a little less to knock it out of an Amish. That bigheadedness got me into problems and, before I was done, I think I caused more trouble than the accidents that had brought people to the hospital in the first place.

We'd been fishing, my dad and I. Being a dumb kid as I was, I figured all the biggest fish were out in the center of the

lake. The only way my line was going to get there was by casting as far as I could. It didn't matter my dad telling me not to
do that; with each cast I was trying harder and harder.

In fact, I was casting so hard I even took my hat off for
more distance. I cranked back and let go one more time. As
Dad stood there waiting to see the splash, I realized I had
managed to put the spinner into the back of my head.

Needless to say, everybody in a five-county area got
pretty excited about this. It didn't really hurt, wasn't bleeding
or anything, and they probably could have worked the hook
out right there. Just to be safe, though, Dad snipped the line
and we headed to the hospital.

One of mankind's oldest games must be the Emergency
Room Game. That's where everybody sits around in a small
room trying to figure out what's wrong with everybody else.
I didn't know anything about the game, but the fat woman
sitting in the chair next to me must have been an old pro.

When I say fat, I'm understating the situation by at least
half. She was using all space possible and then some. She was
none too pleased some squirt of a kid, that being me, would
dare take up a full chair. As she had everybody else in the
room figured out, she started looking us over out of the corner of her eye.

Dad sensed what was going on. Just being the rascal, he
said something that made me turn my head to face him. The
fat woman got one look at that spinner dangling out of my
head, let out a scream and fainted dead away.

I'll tell you, she got immediate service at that. Funny how
all the other English folks would rather stand around the
emergency room than fill that empty chair of hers. I was afraid
they might of had something against Amish people. Maybe
they do. Amish people with fishhooks hanging out of their
heads, at least.

No amount of medicine or doctors can help some,

though. You may have heard, you may have read, that the Amish have inbred, marrying first cousins as long as sixty years ago. That may be one of the few things you've heard about the Amish that's true. Maybe only just now are we seeing the effects. It's a difficult notion to explain other than to tell you about Willie.

Willie is a big kid, about six-foot-four and two hundred twenty pounds, jet-black hair and pale blue eyes. Even though the calendar says he's twenty-four, because of that inbreeding so many generations back, he'll never have the mind of any more than a seven-year-old. Work he can, though, and work he does, especially now that his brothers and sisters have grown and started families of their own.

There never was much problem for Willie to hitch up a team of draft horses, but field work was another matter. Finally, just two years ago, Willie's dad decided it was time to have Willie do some plowing. Time for Willie to grow one more notch in some ways. They got all hitched up, moved the team over to the field and got set to go to work.

"Now Willie, this is what I want," said his dad. "You plow out there to the oak tree, keeping it straight as you can. It's very simple. Can you do that?"

Willie nodded, flicked the lines and off they went. Willie proceeded to plow a furrow so straight a surveyor would of been real proud. He plowed right out to the oak tree, straight out to the tree itself, and then he stopped. And stood there. And stood there.

After about five minutes, the old man decided he'd better find out what was wrong. Our People get curious that way. Out across the field he went, worrying and wondering. He got right up beside Willie and just started to open his mouth when Willie turned to him and said, "Hi, Poppa. Now what?"

When the old man explained about making turns and

doing the whole field, it made sense enough to Willie. Once again he nodded, flicked the lines and was off.

Yoder was still chuckling about his boy's stunt as I pulled up. We got to visiting, looking at the barn stock and eating pie to the point time slipped away. I did want to say hello to Willie before I left, so Yoder and I headed over to the field.

I will always remember walking up to the gate, Yoder letting out with a shriek and then him starting to run across that freshly plowed field. Oh yes, every furrow perfect, as if a master plowman had turned the soil in that field. And then into the next field as well.

Yoder can laugh about it today, and he does sometimes, but it wasn't funny then. Willied had plowed the field all right and, since the gate was open, kept right on going. By the time we got to him, he was three furrows deep into neighbor Old Miller's best pasture, cows dodging for cover and prime grazing ground torn to shreds. Things were pretty tense as we worked until well after dark trying to repair the damage. It took us that long to realize one thing. Willie's dad told him to plow. He never said anything about stopping.

Willie and all like him are what the Amish call God's special children. It's understood these young ones may be frustrating at times but they are a pleasant reminder of a state of innocence, too. They will be cared for until eternity.

Unlike some of our Pennsylvania cousins, Ohio's Amish haven't started up special schools for the disabled yet. Friends of ours up to the north and the west of us, nearer to Berlin, send their special ones to the public training program and that's good. 'Round here, in cases like Willie, we're more partial to home schooling. That's good, too, but in a way, Willie missed out on a most glorious time. That time when every boy and girl discovers there's something beyond this valley. That most joyous discovery is a thing called formal education.

Schooling

When an Amish baby comes into this world, either he is a little woodchopper or she is a little dishwasher. The young one holds that title until about the age of seven. It is then, upon entry into the first grade, that the young assume a new role, that of being a scholar.

It was a long struggle for the Amish to establish their own school systems. Some point to a 1972 United States Supreme Court case involving the state of Wisconsin and a man named Yoder as the landmark decision, but that's not really right. If the truth be known, the words of those justices mirrored what the Ohio Supreme Court had said eleven years before, back in 1961 when they rendered an opinion on a case that began in 1944. That was a long time, but we think the decision ended up being right for everybody.

The Amish don't think themselves better than anybody, but they don't see no need for higher education. The first eight grades are enough and that's what those jurists said, too.

They figured that even if someone would leave the faith, the skills and the work ethic learned as Amish were so valuable they'd never be a burden on society. Those wise judges have been right up until now and we'll keep doing our best to prove them right forever.

I recall a little of those bad old days when it comes to Amish education. We know some of the people who got put in jail for the crime of not sending a child to public school. I call myself a friend to a few who were placed in foster homes, having been denied a "decent upbringing" by being raised Amish. I think all involved will agree that we're glad those days are finally over and that I've said enough as it is.

We've got our own school around here called Valley Ridge. I can't say the name makes too much sense, but a lot of being Amish don't make sense either sometimes. Our teacher there is Arlene Weaver. She's harnessmaker Nelson's second girl, the one Levi's partial to but nobody's suppose to know that. This is her second year and I'd say she enjoys it, although there was one day last fall she had her doubts.

Arlene had read, or heard, that a good way to increase a

scholar's vocabulary is with rhymes. She asked who knew a
word that rhymed with cow, up shot a hand and somebody
said, "Mow." That was very good and the next word was
course. Another hand was up and out came "Horse." One
thing for sure, she should of stopped right there.

Teacher wondered if anybody knew a word that sounded
like wit. Up went Little Amos's hand and he shouted out . . .
well, something.

I understand there was a note sent home to the Yoder
house, but Mrs. Yoder wasn't too hard on Amos. However, I
do know his father, Andy, is a little more careful on what's
said at the supper table these days. I've heard there's all sorts
of words that could come popping into next week's vocabulary lesson.

Of course my own personal start in the educational system would have been traumatic enough for even the bravest
of scholars. On that morning of my first day of being a first
grader at the Hillside School, I received firm instruction that as
soon as school was dismissed that afternoon, I would immediately run to the swings, sit down and wait for my sister to walk
home with me.

It wasn't necessary to repeat those instructions nor did I
argue with my parents as I've seen so many city children do
these days. I listened to the words of my parents because I respected and trusted them. They led by example, not the art of
hypocrisy, and I knew if they said for me to do something, it
was in my best interest that I did. If they had enough trust in
Sis, just a fifth grader at the time, to have her watch out for me,
then I knew I could trust her, too.

As hard as I try, I cannot recall a single event of that first
day in the classroom itself. Those specifics are lost to my
memory completely. It is only when the dismissal bell was
tolled and I made my dash to the swings do the events of the
day come into a very sharp focus.

Indeed I did dash right to those swings. I might not have been the first scholar out the door, but no more than three were leading me. With two hops I was in the swing, anxiously awaiting my sister so I could get right home to share my day.

It seemed like the whole school went by me in a solid mass that afternoon. Even if there were only thirty enrolled in the Hillside School, all their faces blended together in the congregation of children that swept past me. One or two stragglers took a pass or two on the swing, but not for long. No sense in playing if chores were calling. With everybody else gone, I sure did wish Sis would hurry and we could go home.

I don't know how much time had passed, me still sitting on that swing, when Mrs. Troyer came out of the school door and headed for home. Teacher lived some distance from the school, so she drove her buggy even on the nice days. The stable some of the fathers had built for her horse and rig was right near the swings, so it was sort of natural she'd stroll my way to see what I was up to.

Mrs. Troyer seemed relieved that I wasn't having any problem, I was just waiting for someone. We talked a little bit, her being so nice, and she gave me a lot of encouragement. Being a scholar is not an easy task, especially for a first grader. I was feeling pretty good when she took her leave, hitched up her buggy and, with one last wave, headed for her home. A nice lady, but I wished Sis would hurry with her cleaning the blackboards or whatever she was doing.

Probably that would have been a very good time to be giving serious thought to all I'd learned that day. I'm really sorry I can't recall the day for it was quite historic. It was then that I began to learn that most peculiar language, English.

Oftentimes since I've seen strangers come into an Amish community and get all excited at the sight of little ones. The strangers rave about how darling Amish children are, the adorable miniatures of their mothers and fathers. Some strangers even go to the children, they ask how they are or maybe even what the little one's name might be. All they get for an answer is a smile.

The stranger goes off figuring Amish children must be some sort of imbeciles. No, and not even close at that. It's just that the little ones know only the language of the home, a dialect of German called Pennsylvania Deutsch. It's only in the first grade that English begins to open a new, and sometimes strange, world.

It is obvious, even to the most casual observer, that I didn't practice my English that first day of school—or too much after, for that matter. The serious, mechanical side of words and letters just wasn't for me. I was too busy trying to grasp the concept to ever worry about handling any of the details. That's not to say my mind was totally empty, however.

Even at that young age, one of my greatest attributes was a vivid imagination. I watched the birds flying over and speculated on what sort of view of earth they must have. The gray squirrel that came close to the swings would soon be holing up for winter, his home so warm and secure. I saw myself as a bird in flight and a snuggled squirrel, lost in a most pleasant daydream of a life in nature.

According to the family legend, life went right on that afternoon. Near to five that evening, after finishing up the work on a storage shed for neighbor Glick, Dad came walking up our lane heading for supper. Through the back door he went, spying the table all set and the meatloaf just coming out of the oven.

Just like every other evening when he came home from work, Dad would wash up at the pitcher pump over the sink, ask my mother how her day was and then announce he was ready to eat. It was right after that, when my mother told Sis to call me to supper, that the excitement started.

Maybe it was more a case of paralysis at first than excite-

ment. I heard that Sis stopped in her tracks, her face register-
ing first remembrance and then terror. It took a second or two
before my mother realized the situation. I'm told her face
went that same route. By the time Dad got the message, they
left supper stand and went dashing out the door.

I'd never realized Dad could be such a fast driver until
then. Should somebody of ever organized the Peoli 500 for
buggies, I'd estimate the man would of drawn pole position.
That buggy was just about on two wheels when they came
ripping into the school yard that evening. Figuring this meant
it was time to go, I finally left my perch on the swing, walked
over to the buggy, climbed in and asked how everybody was,
being neighborly as I am.

Things were pretty tense that evening. The folks held to
the opinion there was a need for discipline, Amish style. Sis
tasted a couple of licks from Mom's strap and then three
smacks from Dad's hickory switch. I felt bad about her getting
punished, having been so myself in the past on great and rare
occasions—about once a week—but I also wasn't so dumb as
not to savor one benefit of the entire incident.

There never was any worry about me being kidnapped
or the like. We figure the Good Lord's got his eye on little ones
around here. The folks weren't worried about me wandering
off, either. Even then I was Amish enough to mind my man-
ners and mind my folks even more. No, what upset the folks
like you wouldn't believe was that by spending all that time
sitting on a swing, I hadn't gotten my chores done.

The way they saw it that evening, if Sis didn't feel it necessary that I be home after school, then she could handle my
chores for the next week. That notion was so agreeable to me
that I decided I'd mention a thought to Sis that evening as she
fed the chickens for me. The thought, that any time she cared
to leave me at school was fine by me, got mentioned only
once. Sis never said a word or changed expression then or

just a minute later, when she jabbed my backside with the pitchfork.

Certain problems arise from time to time in this quest for higher education. It was in my third-grade year that I learned the way you act at home is not necessarily the way you act in public. At the home place, sitting around the table or the like, if it itched you scratched it. I was admonished privately by Teacher that little boys don't scratch that, at least outside of the outhouse.

It was in the fifth grade when I came in contact with what is known around the world as a school bully. We've always gone for the small, one-room schoolhouse of thirty or so scholars. In such a tiny community it wasn't very hard for this bully to unleash a reign of terror. We all fell into line quickly under the most dire threats, and if any of us dared disobey the bully, we would be depantsed. I'll tell you, it was a great relief to return to school in the sixth grade and find the bully had moved on to another area. To be honest, I've often wondered what ever happened to her.

Valley Ridge is just like all Ohio Amish schools in that it has its own school board. These are fathers of the area who assess the community to keep the school running, pick out the textbooks and hire the teacher. We've had a problem over the years because our teachers have been younger women. They're Amish, that's what we want and all, but they end up getting married and starting a family, changing their own priorities—and rightly so. Things got so desperate before they found Arlene that the school board even asked me to teach a term or two.

It seems that one of the fellows had been talking to my old teacher from Hillside, Mrs. Troyer. He misunderstood when she said, as my name was mentioned as a candidate for the job, that I should have been an astronaut. The fellow assumed, since those space jockeys are sharp cookies, that I must be, too, and that Mrs. Troyer knew something they didn't. Something the whole community was ignorant of, in fact.

Fortunately for all involved, some others checked up on this opinion. Indeed, Mrs. Troyer will always believe me to be a good astronaut. Perhaps the finest in the world. After all, when I was in her class all I ever did was take up space.

Somebody brought the local newspaper for this neck of the woods down to the house the other day. I'd say there wasn't much in all those pages of newsprint that I found interesting other than one most unusual article. It was a strange way to announce what I'd call some really bad news.

According to the story, the public schools around here gave their scholars some sort of standardized test. The idea was to measure how well the scholars were doing in the basics of education and how much they really knew. At first light, it seemed to be a decent enough notion.

When they got all those tests scored, they found that forty-eight percent of the scholars had passed the exam. The newspaper explained that meant forty-eight percent were able to do the minimum level of work acceptable for young folks of that grade. They didn't say this, but if forty-eight percent passed, that says to me fifty-two percent failed.

Down in the Peoli Valley, we don't have the electricity to power all those televisions, radios or computer things. We like to keep all things simple, even our education. Now it could be we really miss out on something by not having all sorts of extracurricular activities or amusement in this life of basics. Could be, and I'll grant you we don't have too much when it comes to convenience. Then again, fifty-two percent of our people don't fail, either. If it's all the same to the rest of the world, we'll just keep doing it our way for a little while longer.

As interesting as school can be for a scholar, by the age of fourteen and the completion of the eighth grade, it is time to put the books aside. The title of scholar is dropped, and the children become known as the young folks. With head up, it's an all-too-quick march into adulthood via the way of work.

It is a mystery to me where some people get the notion that the Amish are some kind of utopians, never chasing after a dollar like everybody else. The Plain People, even the young, may not run after money, but we do move in that direction at a fast trot at least. We may be Amish, but we're still Americans and every one of us has got taxes coming due.

This isn't to say that the Amish children haven't been working before. There's always been chores at home, assigned in the firm belief that a child who learns to work will never want things handed to him, like so many today. I've seen ten-year-olds, Ivan's boy being one of them, who can handle a team of draft horses as good as any man. It's different now, though. The young folks are learning a trade and, more important, earning a dollar or two. Somewhere along the way they're about to discover what being a teenager is all about.

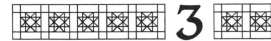 **3**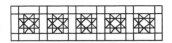

The formative years

When it comes to choosing an occupation for a young fellow, it's a pretty simple affair within the Amish community. About ninety-nine times out of one hundred, you're going to be what your dad is. Every Amish man or woman might be a farmer at heart, but only one man in three has got the land to do so these days in Ohio. The Plain People don't spend much time worrying or regretting about that. There's plenty of other options just around the corner.

I had it pretty easy myself, being an only son. My dad was a builder and so am I. Grandpa was a builder, too, and right there just might be my greatest regret in life. I didn't listen enough and he passed away before I was smart enough to use my ears more than my mouth. When Grandpa died, one of the world's greatest talents ceased to be.

All Grandpa needed was some lumber, a saw, a tape measure, a level, a mallet, a slick, an auger and a little rope. With those tools and supplies, he could build a barn. The

whole barn, thank you, in that post-and-beam style. I heard
some even pay these days to learn that skill, and me, I just
didn't listen. At least it keeps me humble, being so dumb.

Leroy, that string bean of a fellow up the way, doesn't
have it so simple, trying to pass on a trade. He was a farmer,
so the first two boys learned that way of life. More children
were coming along, so Leroy retired from farming and laid
concrete block. After he taught that to two more sons, he retired to making wooden pallets. Now that two of the boys are
doing that for a living, I've heard some say he just retired
again to open a sawmill. Talk's already in the area that he's
planning the next retirement to start a woodworking shop.
One thing for sure, by the time he gets through the next five
boys, Leroy will have retired enough to build, clothe and feed
his own subdivision.

With all this hand-me-down work, it strikes me odd how many different jobs there are in the Amish community. There's the farmers and the builders, but there's a whole lot of fellows making garage doors these days in a big factory. Buggy-makers, blacksmiths and harnessmakers, too, but more than one is making bricks for another big corporation. There's even an Amish tax adviser these days, one sharp fellow. Industrious people, but keeping food on the table and the tax man away is getting to be a full-time job anymore.

Things are a little simpler for the girls of a family because they are planning on becoming what their mothers are—housewives. That has been, is and always will be the predominant Amish occupation for women. The girls will put the skills they learned at their mother's apron to good use and make someone very happy someday. Before they do, though, there's nothing wrong with using those skills to make a dollar or two, even if it does involve a real collision of worlds.

There was a family south of us, down toward Kimbolton, that needed a maid. They're English, but that has nothing to do with Great Britain. To be Amish is to see the world real clear. You're either Unser Leit (Our People, the Amish) or else you're English (the English speakers). At any rate, they put an ad in the paper and the very next day, here comes Carol.

Carol's a good Amish girl, those brown eyes that's got a permanent twinkle in them, and her poppa thought it a good idea she work awhile, earning a little money of her own. This family, the James family, and Carol struck a deal and she had the job.

In no time flat, Carol had that house spotless. Dust was just not allowed to exist. She was such a good worker that she could even mind the small children, too, being a nanny as well as a maid. Some would say the family was getting two employees for the price of one. Others might say that Fred and his family got a little more than they bargained for. With Carol being such a good worker, the family had no problem with her until they realized there was a little quirk to Carol.

About once a week or so, Carol's back would hurt her. Hurt her so bad she couldn't scrub the floors that day. She could iron, though, if that was all right. In fact, she could set the ironing board up in the living room, do her pressing work and watch the small children at the same time. With Carol being such a good worker, the family had no problem with the request.

It was six scorched shirts later before Fred and his wife discovered what was going on. The Ordnung, that is, the rules of Carol's congregation, were clear that she could not own a television. In fact she couldn't even turn one on and watch, but should somebody else flip the switch, there wasn't anything in the rules about watching it then. Somehow it had been mentioned that if the children would want the television on, that was fine. Carol became so engrossed in the show that she then burned right through Fred's shirts.

Other arrangements have now been made. Carol comes to work an hour earlier each day. She works hard, harder than ever. In fact, she works so hard that she earns an hour's rest every afternoon. Right at the time something called *General Hospital* comes on. Three years and she hasn't missed an episode yet.

Those lures of the city are easy to understand. I recall many years ago, when I was just five, going into town with my dad. Those were earlier times and we didn't have indoor plumbing, nor had I ever seen it before. You can imagine the fascination for a young man to pull a lever and water came rushing down. Naturally I pulled it again, and again, and again everywhere I could until I was dragged out of that most amazing room twenty minutes later by Dad.

For whatever reason, I didn't go back into that particular

store for more than twenty years. I happened to saunter in one day, though, and there was the old man who had run it so many years before, still standing behind the counter.

"Hey," he said as I walked in, "you come to buy something or do you want to play with the toilets again?" Just living proof, I'd suppose, that a man can never escape his past.

Life would be a dull affair if all there was to look forward to was work. Being a teenager confined to a life of drudgery would be a terrible fate. It makes me glad the Amish don't take to that notion. We've got our own ideas about being a teenager. Around here it's called *rumspringa,* the running-around years. That's when you try it all to see what it's all like, with the knowledge that nine times out of ten you'll come back where you belong.

It's a fact, ever since time began for the Amish, I imagine, that some carry on like wild heathen. They pull just about every stunt in the book, and then those in the revised edition of the book as well. Buggymaker John even moved to New York City when he was seventeen and I know he must of at least seen it all. Nothing for sure, but he certainly does grin whenever the Big Apple is mentioned. Why, some young folks even go so far as to buy an automobile, hiding it at a neighbor's or at the local gas station.

One fellow did just that, bought a car for $762.32 and kept it down the way at the service station. Oh, could he impress the guys and the girls, too, with that two-toned 1968 Buick Special with air-conditioning, 350 V-8 engine, AM radio and automatic transmission. The one he especially wanted to impress, though, was the little dark-haired beauty named Rachel, who was about as wild as he was.

Somehow this fellow and Rachel ended up sitting in that car one afternoon on the hilltop overlooking the Peoli Valley. They did their share of talking and such until just before dark. They'd had the gravel lane, not even much of a road, to themselves all that time until they saw a buggy coming slowly up the hill behind them.

The buggy pulled right up beside the car and stopped. Very slowly the canvas side curtain was raised and the stately white beard of Levi Swartzentruber appeared. It was a tense moment, for not only was he a pillar of the church, Levi was also Rachel's uncle. To say hearts were pounding was the understatement of the year.

The old man waited until the car driver nodded in greeting and then said, "Do you mind a piece of advice, boy?" The young fellow shook his head, bracing himself for a stern lecture at the very best.

"When you kiss her, keep your foot off the brake pedal. My wife and I were sitting down below on the front porch of the home place thinking you were flashing some sort of Morse Code at us."

With that he dropped the curtain, made a U-turn with the buggy and headed for home. The only way this story can end is for me to tell you I had that car sold the very next Monday morning.

I'd suppose if there were one hundred Amish young people in a room, they could recount one hundred ways to savor the *rumspringa* time. Little Joe probably wishes he'd of bought a Buick; he invested in alcohol instead and ended up with a blood alcohol level of .25, a night in jail and a fine for drunk driving. Buggy driving at that.

Even our English friends have made a little game of this Amish experience. I understand up at Creston they have some sort of homecoming festival every year. The fellows who run the games like to play "Let's See Who's Trying Not to Look Amish Tonight" every year. The young folks who frequent the carnival don't seem to be able to figure out how those English are so smart, but I'm getting a hunch myself.

Maybe it's because a young fellow is wearing broadfall

trousers, the kind that close with five buttons, not a zipper. Possibly the young lady didn't tie her scarf just right and her prayer cap is showing. Perhaps her long dress is a clue as well, or maybe that her boyfriend's haircut was done with a bowl and scissors. It's either that or the fact the Amish kids are running around speaking Deutsch that makes the Plain People stand out. All for the sake of carrying out, and carrying on, this old Amish tradition.

This is a growing community hereabouts and not just from young folk marrying and starting families. Maybe every other year we'll get immigrants, Amish from other areas of Ohio looking for cheaper land or a little more space. With each new family come new ideas, doing some things the way they did it back in Hardin County or wherever. I heard some newcomer boys use those cars they've got so carefully hidden to go as far as that amusement place, Cedar Point.

Some may be critical but I'm not among them. It's not that I'd care to see that place, for I don't, but I do have a pretty good memory of my *rumspringa*. For us, we did our adventuring in the hidden car to a place called Chippewa Lake.

It just happened some of us were up that way a short time back, going to the auction at Creston. As the sale wasn't that much and we had some time, we decided to go the last ten miles and see what that scene of so many good times looked like these days.

Maybe you can imagine my surprise as we rounded the last bend to discover that the park's still there, but it's not open anymore. We went up to the gate, all padlocked shut, to get a closer look. I think every one of us in the van had some memory of the place. Lester was talking of the fun house, Marvin raving about that speedboat they used to run on the lake. For me, I sure liked that roller coaster. Scared me to death and I couldn't wait to get back on it. It was real strange, looking at it now.

As we were gawking through the fence, a car pulled up and a young lady got out. We were thinking at first she might tell us to be moving on, but far from it. She lives right close by the park, in one of those cottages by the lake. She's so wild about the place she even wrote a book about the park.

From what she said, folks used to come there even before the Civil War to picnic and have a good time. As she was talking about those good times and famous people who came there, I got to thinking back a few years. It was fun to go to the park, good clean fun. There wasn't no drinking or carrying on like some places. A family place, didn't need to spend a lot of money and it sure left a good feeling when you headed for home each night.

Instead of that good feeling looking at a place so beautiful, I got to feeling real empty, seeing what used to be. It was like an old friend had slipped away. I think it was Lester who asked this lady if she thought the place would ever open up again. I was feeling a little better when she said it just could be. Somebody always seemed to be interested lately and the grand old lady of amusement parks just might wake up again. She sure was trying hard enough.

It was right about then that the biggest flock of Canada geese I'd ever seen came flying right over us. You could hardly hear for the honking as they settled in on Chippewa Lake. That's about the most beautiful music in the world to me, but this time it caused my mind to play tricks on me.

I could almost hear the wheels of the roller coaster cars again. A band was playing up in that magnificent ballroom. There was laughter, even if it was only in my mind, coming from people having a good time. That was a good memory to hand on to the next generation. Seeing a place like that come back to life is a hope worth holding on to as well.

My wallet was out without a second thought and I said, "I'll take one of your books if you've got one." I was well pleased to buy one, just yesterday thumbing through my copy again to relive a most pleasant time. Maybe it wasn't wild enough for some of these computer-addicted ones today, but it was all the enjoyment I could handle.

With all the mischief some can find these days, I wish that lady well in getting a decent place back on the map. Take the padlocks off, lady, and you'll see a little fellow with reddish brown hair and china blue eyes strolling down Park Drive again. Those aren't empty words Mrs. Kraynek, that's a fact.

When it comes to running around, though, I'd say Jake got a little too far carried away in his *rumspringa*. I don't know what all he did, nor do I want to. He was a good kid before and he is a good one now. Those who love to gossip don't find a warm welcome here. I do know one night he was out joy riding with some English kids in a car. They were going down Old 23 and going too fast.

The car went off the road in a pretty bad crash. One was killed and Jake, well, we didn't know for a long time. He was in the hospital for three months, then bedridden at home for six more. The steady stream of visitors he'd had in the hospital became a flood at home. Everybody wishing good cheer and such, but one visitor really bothered them.

This fellow only came once, even though some could say he is that family's most loyal friend. He's the kind who's always clowning around, telling jokes and stories, but he didn't have much to say when he came to see Jake. He just sat like he was thinking about his own wild days. How close he'd come to disaster himself. It didn't make sense to the family, this change in character, but it doesn't matter. I only hope Jake's family never finds out how much I really love them.

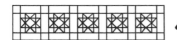 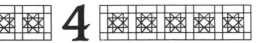

A matter of faith

It's been about two months now since Wild Jake was baptized into the congregation. The running-around years are over, at least for him. He's an adult now, having made a sacred vow to follow the rules of the congregation, that Ordnung I mentioned, for life. It is the most serious decision in his life, for he knows it is far better never to make his vow than to make it and later break it. To break his vow with the congregation leaves no choice other than to come under the mite, or what you might have heard called a shunning.

Some say there are thirteen kinds of horse-and-buggy Amish in Ohio today. Nowhere is the shun as serious as down in the Peoli Valley. Here you will neither buy nor sell, nor eat nor drink, nor even speak with one who has fallen away. It's brutal, it's vicious and it's a fact of Amish life, but it always struck me strange it didn't seem to bother Mose when they ran his boy out of the area.

Run him out we did, and I mean all of us, for he thought for himself. He read and he wondered, questioning everything and even daring to laugh once in a while at how silly we all can be. Such behavior didn't sit well and it didn't sit at all when he went out and started courting an English girl. In fact some just about choked on it.

They gave him three chances to bring her into our fold, but he wouldn't have it. It was her world he wanted to live in forever, not his. Jonas knew the shunning was coming so he didn't even show up to church that Sunday. I'd suppose he didn't see any need to be a whipping boy one more time. He'd already said his good-byes to his real friends and was long gone.

Maybe I just didn't give it too much thought until last February. We was all to Columbus to the big draft horse auction when I noticed Mose wasn't too interested in the horses. He was acting real peculiar, checking the time a lot until about noon. Just about then he decided to ease away from the crowd.

For whatever reason, one of those little voices in the back of my mind told me to investigate, that I just might learn something. Playing that hunch, I followed Mose at a distance. He wandered around a little bit to throw off any suspicion and then made a beeline to a pay phone. I watched him fish out a quarter, tap out a well-known number and for the next half hour had himself quite a conversation.

I don't know what was said, but as he hung up and turned around, Mose had a grin that has been reserved for grandpas since time began. For a little while longer, the world was just fine to him. For one more year, things were all right. Sure, his boy was run out for wanting another kind of life, but he's still blood. We might of run him out of the valley but never from Mose's heart and that's just fine by me.

Perhaps more than in any other church, the rite of baptism is a passage into adulthood for the Amish. Baptism is more than the outward sign of a woman changing her style of cape and shawl or a man growing his beard. It is an acceptance of, and by, a fellowship of believers and the true beginning into a lifetime of heavenly service.

Back in 1525, when a group called the Swiss Brethren was formed, infant baptism was the norm. The Brethren, our forefathers of the plain church, didn't go for that, and some other things as well. They figured only an adult could make the choice to follow Christ and so do we.

We figure if a young man or woman has got a career lined up, has shown a good moral character and survived his or her running-around years, it's time to join the fold. Time to come into a society of believers not for an hour, not for a week, but for eternity. Amish people hope the young choose wisely, letting our Lord guide their decision. Once in a great, great while, though, there's been a mistake or two.

A few years before I came into this world, a fellow was excommunicated from a Wayne County congregation. Instead of accepting his church's decision, this fellow took his affairs to a court of law. He sued his bishop and preachers, demanding they not only stop the shunning but pay him damages as well.

Not being much for the legal system, the Amish holy men didn't put up much of a defense. Their argument was that our faith is one of tradition, that we are bound together by holding to basic principles. For our people, we find contentment in security. Coupled with our tradition goes the confidence that our neighbors think as we do. Through our support of one another and faith in the Lord, we will survive even as pilgrims in a most strange land.

Unfortunately the legal system put more stock in the rights of the individual over the good of a community. The convenience of one individual couldn't be sacrificed even if it threatened the good of the congregation. The judge awarded damages and ordered the congregation to stop shunning. In fact, he declared the act of the shun itself to be illegal.

Well, the fellow got the money he wanted and I really do hope he enjoyed every penny of it. Funny thing, though, he stayed shunned, and all Amish continue to shun to this day. For a while longer we'll keep supporting the Constitution of the United States. We won't tell Uncle Sam how to run his business and he won't tell us what language to pray in. With that we'll call it even.

It always tends to surprise me how people can misperceive the Amish. It seems what dumbfounds most folks is that the theology of the Amish is exactly the same as a Methodist, Baptist or any other Protestant faith. It has to be because the Amish are a branch of the second oldest Protestant religion. The Lutherans, followers of Martin Luther who got the ball rolling around 1517, are the first, but if you look close, the Swiss Brethren who became the Anabaptists who became the Mennonites from whom the Amish pulled away aren't too far behind.

It's not the issues of theology but the interpretation that draws the Amish out. The Plain People put great stock in not being worldly. We don't dress different or do things different to stand out from the crowd. We want to stand *away* from the crowd. It's not that electricity and the car are sinful, but what they can bring into a home is. We'd far prefer to stay away from that and take support from each other, from the people we've learned all our lives to trust.

To understand an Amish congregation, you've got to see

all those baptized men and women as a base, a rock that the church is built on. A big, wide base that might have two hundred individuals molded into a strong unit. All in agreement and all in support, and from this base the leadership of the church is drawn.

A scholar of organizations, one of those professors of social groups or the like, would have an easy chart to draw if he'd come and study our church. At the top is our bishop, then three preachers, the deacon and then the congregation. If it seems simple, there's a very good reason for that. It is.

We, like all Amish congregations, live by the adage that if you want to keep your holy men humble, don't pay them very much. If that be true, Amish churchmen are the humblest on earth because we don't pay them at all. Levi, the one I see quite a bit at the mill, is our bishop. Among the preachers we've got a carpenter, a roofer and a farmer. Our deacon is retired, but nobody ever retires from serving our Lord. These are lifetime hobbies, as it were, performed with a cheerful heart.

Just because this is the way we do it down Peoli way doesn't mean that's the way it is in Baltic or Plain City or elsewhere. You might find two congregations sharing a bishop here, a congregation with just two preachers there. That's because there's no such thing as a conference or association of all Amish churches. The last time I checked, there were nearly two hundred fifty Amish congregations in Ohio alone. That makes for a possibility of two hundred fifty ways of doing things. It's not that bad, but at times it's not far from it.

One of the funny things I hear English say is that Amish is Amish, they're all the same. All the horse-and-buggy crowd being one big happy family. In actuality there have been thirteen separate groups formed these last eighty years out of that family. A bishop, or bishops, will take exception to the norm, lead a flock out on their own thinking, and a new branch of the Amish tree is formed. With just a few exceptions, these offshoots will be named for the bishop or for their locale.

Most folk have heard of the Old Order and they are the most common. Some know of the New Order, the ones on rubber-rimmed buggy wheels, as well. There are even a few outsiders aware of the Swartzentruber Amish, the conservative ones. Sometimes I think it's sad how little folks do know. Other times, it's just as well they don't understand for they'd end up as confused as we are.

If you made a list of the Amish styles in Ohio, you'd have to include King, Dan Miller, New Order, Old Order, Chesterhill, Tobe Hostettler, Andy Weaver, Roman Miller, Stutzman Troyers, Swartzentruber Number Ones and Number Twos, Sam Yoders and last, but not least, the bottom of the barrel, Peolis. That's not us, that's our neighbors, but more on them later.

Thirteen factions that are no more than frameworks those two-hundred-fifty-some congregations could fit into. Just because one Old Order congregation does things one way doesn't mean every one does. The factions dress differently, have different buggy accessories and accept different degrees of technology. It's absolutely a confusion, even to the buggy crowd. There is one thing for sure that comes out of this mess. If you ever hear somebody saying this is the way the Amish do something, lumping us all together, you know he don't know what he's talking about.

Mervin and I were to town not long ago, down to the library I think it was, where a woman was giving a speech about the Amish. The people in charge of the program said it was all right if we sat in, as long as we didn't say anything. Something about not starting a commotion was what they kept bringing up. It bothered me that they were being so insistent on this, bothered me a lot until I heard the woman talk.

She talked for over an hour and I think I heard her get three things right. I'd suspect she'd read an old, outdated book about the Amish and driven through the area once. Mervin got fed up with the stupidity of it and left, but I stuck it out, figuring it would get better. I made it all the way up to where she said that the quaintest, the most charming of all the factions of the Amish were the ones called the Swartzentrubers. Back home we've got another name for them. We call them dumb, ignorant hillbillies.

I don't mean to be going off on a tangent, but I've held it long enough. There's just some people I can't get along with and our hillbilly neighbors are among them. Some of our neighbors started out as Swartzentruber Amish and they only got worse. I don't mean to be better than anybody and I try to be humbler than most. It just irritates me to no end that some think not only are all Amish the same, we're all a bunch of friends.

There's some kin of mine in this bunch but I'm not real proud of it. From Easter to Thanksgiving, they're all going barefoot. Their farms are pigpens, they themselves aren't often acquainted with the bathtub, and whereas the Amish in general average seven children to a household, this bunch averages twelve. They're out at night without a slow-moving-vehicle sign, they speak English rarely and some think it's still the year 1800. Some haven't even caught up to that time yet.

Joseph, one of these hillbillies, was going to be a farmer once. It came one summer and they were working the threshing crew. Somehow the machine got jammed. Joseph jumped back there and, when it got cleared, somehow the bar came down and severed his leg.

They rushed around, some running over to get the neighbors to come and others pouring kerosene over Joe's leg. Believe it or not, the kerosene's not too bad. A very soothing effect and it does prevent shock. At any rate, it wasn't but a few minutes later when the neighbor arrived in his truck.

They rushed off to County Hospital, but they couldn't reattach the leg. The best the doctors could do was get Joe stabilized. When the family was sure he'd be all right, they loaded him and his severed leg up and went home.

This bunch then proceeded to go out to the family cemetery and bury Joe's leg. They believe that if you do that, the victim will be free from the pain that comes with amputation. The problem was Joe still had pain.

They then went out, dug the leg up, turned it over and reburied it. Joe doesn't have any more pain.

Then there's people, English people I'm speaking of, who think just because you're named Swartzentruber you must be a Swartzentruber Amish. Old Eli's just about ready to shoot the next one who says that. Swartzentruber Amish followed first Bishop Sam Yoder and then two Bishop Swartzentrubers away from the Old Order years ago. Just sometimes seems like nobody takes the time to learn anymore.

Thinking about those neighbors got me so upset that I got way off course. We were talking about the organization of the Amish church, the bishop on down to the body of believers known as the congregation. Even though I mentioned that all the holy positions were a lifetime calling, one thing I've neglected is our somewhat unique selection process known as the lot.

Let's say one of our preachers passed away or decided to move to Wisconsin. At the next communion service, which is held once in the spring and once in fall, the wheels start turning to select a new man to lead and represent the congregation. Using a combination of democracy and divine intervention, the congregation will make sure of its survival.

The election will be held with all baptized members, men

and women alike, of the congregation voting. Should a man
receive three or more votes, he's placed into what's called the
lot. Once the lot is assembled, at that same service, they will
retire to another room. In that room is one Ausbund, the
church hymnbook, for each man. As the spirit moves each
one in his own way, every man will select a book. Should the
hymnal selected have a single piece of paper inside, that man
has become the new preacher of the congregation.

Things were done different around here until just a short
time ago. We had a unique custom regarding the lot, not waiting until the next communion but getting right on with it as
soon as possible. I never gave it much thought, figuring if
we'd done it that way for a long time, it must be all right.

As a matter of fact, I was one of the last to agree a change
would be appropriate. Just because most, if not all, Amish
congregations do it this way was a fine reason, but not fine
enough for me. I might have stayed against the revision but
for a visit from Mose, the deacon of our church.

Mose came visiting, in the spirit of friendship and to give
me a lesson in local history. The Amish who first came to
Ohio ended up in the Holmes County area. The community
grew, spreading out from time to time. Some ended up in
Plain City before the turn of the century, others up in Geauga
County. Our local people didn't start showing up in this neck
of the woods until about 1950.

I was born here and always figured it was just a nice
place some found and took to one day. Listening to Mose talk
about those times clued me in that those were less than ideal
times. He knew firsthand and figured I'd like to hear about
some things that haven't been discussed much the last forty
years.

It seems that during World War II and for a few years
after, some county officials up north believed it their duty to

force Amish children into public schools. It got real ugly, some Amish parents being put in jail and their children placed into foster homes. Noah L. Hershberger of Wisconsin even wrote a book called *Struggle to Be Separate* about the whole situation. I've read that text and would recommend it in a second, but I never dreamed it was the school problem that caused us to be here.

Certainly it could be true, and we would hope that it is, that those county officials were just doing their job. Given the public trust, they were simply interpreting the letter of the law. They wanted what was right and best for everybody. That reasoning is by far preferable to another logic, that when these prosecutions began it just happened to be 1944.

History says that in 1944 the people of these United States were fighting a very popular war. The threat of imperial Japan and the Nazis was all so real. Right in the middle of all this war fervor stood the Amish, conscientious objectors to the use of violence to resolve any conflict. Perhaps it could be that some, when given the public trust, chose to punish those who didn't march off to the so-called glory of killing another human being.

Where some become confused is when they lump conscientious objectors with deserters. Again, people not taking the time to understand the situation. Amish people serve, but not in combat or combat-related duties. An obligation to fulfill to this great country is not a problem for the pleasure of living in the United States. I would suppose that it's just some don't understand others' beliefs, and maybe don't try to, either.

Some around here were drafted during the Viet Nam conflict but, unlike so many others, they thought it a pretty good idea to go to service. They went to a C.O. outfit, doing hospital work. Funny as it may seem, at the same time there were all sorts of fellows who were C.O.s as long as any chance of being killed in that war existed. Once the shooting stopped, their peacefulness was going right out the window. Well, Amish people don't work that way. We live our conviction every day, but that's our business, to live a life not on convenience but righteousness. Those other fellows didn't ever understand the Amish wanting to do C.O. service.

It's a fact, though, that the local boys were real happy to be changing linens and bedpans eight hours a day. It wasn't for the pay or the veterans' benefits they never claimed that they labored so hard. It was for the next eight hours after each shift of work. That eight hours they spent watching television in the hospital lobby.

These thoughts came racing back to me as Mose kept talking about the court cases, fines and judgments levied against the Amish in those days. There was a lot of fear as the 1940s came to a close. It was that fear that brought our bunch down this way, hoping with some miles between here and all that trouble, cooler heads just might prevail.

Mose's words made a lot of sense all of a sudden. Our congregation had lived in fear of a modern persecution for nearly forty years. We'd ordained holy men as soon as possible to represent us should the law come knocking. What I was thinking was tradition was just our way of protection. When I got to recalling how good the English have been to us around here, I knew those bad days were behind us. With no reason to be looking over our shoulders anymore, I told Mose I'd be voting to bring us in line with everybody else on this policy the next Sunday.

This notion of a vote and then selection within the lot is the same process by which a deacon is selected. It runs true of selecting a bishop as well, except there's no vote by the congregation. One of those two, three or four preachers will be taking the job. It is a tremendous responsibility, one of many reasons all Amish are up on their Bibles at all times, but one never shirked. There has yet to be a man return from the lot who didn't comment the heart was pounding but the hands were cool.

Where a lot of people get confused is when they think the authority of a congregation rests solely with these men who have been chosen by the lot. That's not really the way it is. These fellows simply make sure the body of believers stays as one within a set of rules the congregation, not the bishop or anybody else, has decided on.

Twice a year, spring and fall, two weeks prior to communion, Amish congregations meet and confirm their rules for living. That's the Ordnung that's been mentioned before here and in any number of other books. It's a rare time that change slips in. Believe it or not, some people in the United States are quite happy as they are.

The Ordnung is thorough, covering a lot of ground. The rules are set for clothing, what technology is acceptable, buggy style, even down to household furnishings. There's nothing left to doubt by the time the congregation, in a unanimous vote, approves another six months of structure. Without that unanimous vote, there'll be no communion two weeks later. We see that sign of fellowship as pretty important, believe me.

Just because there may be a lot of rules doesn't mean the Amish are so rigid they can't breathe. The Ordnung is like a fence around a field. We're the field, the Good Word the seed. If we stay in the fence, let brotherhood cultivate the good and thrive under the light of our Lord, things have a habit of working out just fine. May not be exactly as we'd like, but the Lord knows best. However, there is one small problem with such a complete set of rules.

As we saw with Carol, her iron and the television incident, once the rules of a congregation's Ordnung are set, so then are the exceptions to those rules. I've got cousins in a congregation near Mount Eaton and it's real clear in that neck of the woods. Ever since anybody can remember, their Ordnung has clearly stated they cannot have electrical wires come into the home, aren't permitted to own a telephone and, in no way, are to own a mechanically powered vehicle.

That's the rules and, yes indeed, that's what they live with. You'll not find an electrical wire at Andy's, but you would find a portable generator instead to run those power tools of his and that Hoover vacuum of Mary's. The phone

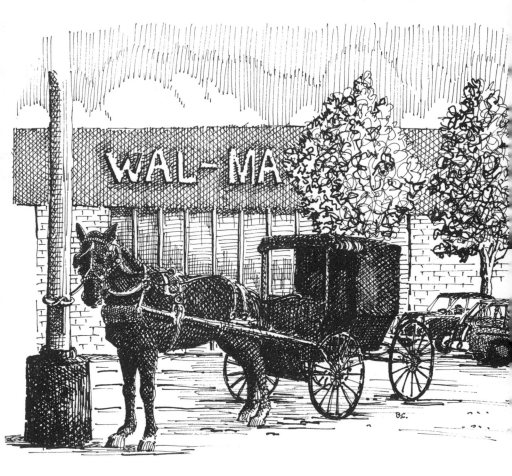

company owns the pay phone on the corner of their lot, not them, but that's nothing compared to what I saw last June when I happened to be in Walnut Creek.

Here comes Andy driving a fairly new pickup truck right into the gasoline station. Not riding in it, driving it. It was against my better judgment, but I had to go over and find out what was going on.

"Hey, I don't own it," said Andy. "I lease it."

I'm sure there's Baptists, Methodists, Jews and probably Moslems pulling the same stunt. Religion is great, just as long as it stays convenient. The way I see it, the own-versus-lease option on that pickup is an issue of Andy's conscience. What I did today I'll sleep with tonight and live with tomorrow. Up to now, for forty-plus years, I've been a real sound sleeper and I plan on keeping it that way.

Ivan claims we all go to church all the time because there's no collection plate. That might be true for some, but the majority does really take to such a gathering. Everybody must really enjoy this, especially when you consider how different this gathering can be.

Amish church runs about four hours every other Sunday. Like so much else with Our People, the four hours and the every other Sunday are a matter of tradition. Just the way we've always done it. Throw in the fact that those four hours are on a backless bench and I don't think too many outsiders care for such an uncomfortable religion.

The ideal size for an Amish congregation would be twenty-six families. That way each home place could have church once a year. Around here we're just beyond perfect, now having thirty-two families in our area, with church making its full circle in about fourteen months anymore.

It was our turn to hold the gathering last month. I knew it but didn't give it a lot of thought until that Tuesday before service was to be. When I got in from pounding nails that evening, I saw Deacon Mose had been by with the green box wagon and it was time to get to work on the home front.

The green wagon is how we get church supplies from one site to the next. All Mose does is pick it up from the last service's locale and drive it over to the next place of worship. It's left to the homeowner to unload the folding benches and boxes of hymnals and then load them back up the week after service. That would be fine if that's all there was to it. Having Amish church requires a lot more, let me tell you.

The first order of business around these parts is to get all the furniture out of the way to make space. Then it's bucket-of-water, on-your-knees-scrubbing, corner-cleaning time. If it can't be cleaned by the scrub brush, then it gets a run through the washing machine. If not washed, then it's painted. The next few days are definitely not the time to be coming in the back door with muddy boots.

It wasn't until Saturday that the house had reached the spotless stage where I could start hauling in the benches. We've got eighty of them in our wagon, me unloading each one, carrying it into the house, unfolding the legs and then getting it placed. It doesn't sound like much and, if I had a full day to do it all, it wouldn't be. The problem was I had to rush, having one more afternoon chore for us to have a real church gathering on Sunday.

I'd imagine the grocery store down toward town loves it when the Amish get together for fellowship. As we were not only having services but also expected to feed the group, I found myself pretty well cleaning out some of their shelves. Sixty pounds of chunk bologna, thirty pounds of Swiss cheese, thirty-five loaves of bread, three cases of pickles and fifteen pounds of coffee later and I was headed for home with the sun going down. Unfortunately, the work wasn't done yet.

It was well after midnight before the last of the bologna had been sliced up and everything else ready. All this work's not for me. I'd far prefer to raise a barn every day than all these chores when it comes to being tired. Still, for the chance to fellowship with our community, Our People, it's well worth it.

The warm weather had come our way that Sunday. With the windows open and a pleasant breeze flowing, it felt downright comfortable sitting on that pew the next morning. It was sort of peaceful and relaxed as Andy launched into the main sermon. Funny, just a few minutes into it and his words seemed to all jumble together to me.

If my head would have fallen so my chin was on my chest, there might not have been any problem. Some claim it was pure chance, while I think I had some help, but it's still a fact my head went back instead. As it went back, my mouth fell open and the snoring started. Not only started but, as I'm told, got louder as Andy preached.

To his credit, Levi delivered one of the most memorable benedictions in the history of our congregation. His words were so memorable that they, or Ivan's elbow in my ribs, roused me from the depths of slumber and left a lasting impression in my mind.

"Sometimes the Word of God is meant to inspire us. Other times it can give us rest. Whichever it be, may each and every one of us not have to stay up too late getting ready for church. Amen." Amen is right to that one.

There are a few good books floating around that can clue you in on the particulars of how a service among the Amish is conducted in detail. I thumbed through some by a fellow named Stephen Scott, finding myself nodding along with what he shared. That man is a writer, making the cloudy points crystal clear. Just the one to tell how a hymn from the Aus-

bund or Liedersammlung can last for thirty minutes. How the
deacon reads not a verse or two, but whole chapters of Scripture. What they can't tell you, though, is what happens when
an Amish congregation gets a windy preacher.

Services down home had been stretching closer to five
hours than four when Preacher Ben came to see John up the
way. It was obvious, even from the start, that Ben was con-
cerned that he might be carrying on too long.

At the same time, it was just as obvious that John wasn't
going to be too direct. He was dealing with the Word of God,
after all. Back and forth they went, Ben wanting to hear John's
opinion and John not wanting to step on toes, especially the
Lord's.

Finally, in exasperation, Preacher Ben said, "John, I do
not mind if a man takes out his pocket watch to check the
time as church goes on. What I do mind is when he takes it
out, checks the time and then shakes it to see if it's still
running."

It's been noted among the congregation that the preach-
ing has been shorter of late. John, he just smiles, but he also
doesn't bring his watch to church anymore, either.

Now there may be some of those young fellows who
were recently baptized who pay attention to every word of
the church service every time we meet. Could be they reflect
on the message for the next thirteen days as well. Could be,
but I'd doubt it myself if they do, especially if they be between
the ages of sixteen and twenty-five. As memory serves me,
there was something else preying on my mind as a newly baptized survivor of the running-around years. I'm not sure what
the English call it, but in Amish country what those teenagers
tend to concentrate on is something we call romance.

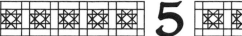 **5**

Romance

If anybody was to be a scholar of Amish ways, wanting to specialize in that area of study called Finding a Mate in the Plain Community, there's only one word to keep in mind. Backwards. It's just that simple: think of an English courtship, turn it one hundred eighty degrees and you just might find love, Amish style.

Romances among the buggy crowd actually begin on a Sunday evening. At the home or in the barn where church had been that morning, the single folk begin to assemble near to seven o'clock to hold what's called a Singing. The theory of this gathering is that the fellows line one side, the girls the other, and everybody fellowships by singing good, pious church songs. That's the theory, but sometimes there's some unique interpretations to the theory as well.

Maybe it's been near to fifty years now since an English fellow decided to investigate this Singing notion. Armed with a real quiet camera of some sort, he managed to slip into a barn in Pennsylvania where there was such a gathering. When his initial shock subsided, he managed to get a picture of the festival. Sure enough, theory and practice were something different.

According to this photo, several of the young fellows were enjoying a cold beer, just as if they were in a cocktail lounge—from what I've heard those places look like. A few of the girls were savoring a cigarette. Most important, there in the center of the barn floor was a radio and several couples were in the process of dancing the jitterbug. Harmless fun, but not quite what most folks would expect at a hymn conference.

This always bothered me, more for always missing such wild times than anything else. We'd always played our gather-

ings pretty straight. It bothered me so much I asked a neighbor, Freeman, if his wife ever danced the jitterbug at a Singing. They're both from a congregation north of here and I was thinking they might know something I don't. After all, Freeman and the wife even went to the Grand Canyon for a vacation once.

"Nope," he said, stroking his beard and trying to appear the wise one, "she did not. But she could dance the pony and the stroll with the best of them."

What I always found amazing about our Peoli Valley Singings was the loss of memory they inspired. That's true, for I cannot recall a single time when at least one young lady did not find herself absolutely helpless. How peculiar it was. The young lady had hitched up her buggy, driven to the Singing, unhitched, gone in and had a very good time. Somehow, though, in all that excitement, she had magically forgot how that horse gets hitched again when she's leaving. Funny how she was always real particular about who helped, too.

At any rate, romance begins and instantly steps behind a wall of secrecy. There's Amish all over Ohio and Pennsylvania and I can't speak for none except down home. I can tell you that the Central Intelligence Agency and the Federal Bureau of Investigation combined would be proud of all the precautions taken just to make sure your business stays your own.

Let's say it's the next Saturday evening after a Singing. It's near six o'clock, suppertime in the Amish world, and the family has gathered at the table. In walks the young man of the house, in his Sunday clothes, and makes like there's nothing out of the ordinary. Sometime through the meal, he'll mention he's figuring on going to town on business.

Nothing will be said about this, even though every place of business has closed an hour before. At least the old folks now know why the young fellow spent the entire afternoon alternating between washing the buggy and combing his hair. They also know that in another house nearby there is a young lady, also in her Sunday clothes, making the announcement she'll be taking a walk this evening. There may be a blizzard outside, but this walk can't wait until tomorrow.

Sure enough, shortly before dark, she'll be standing at a crossroads out of sight from both houses. Just standing, minding her own business and hoping the rest of the world minds its. Sure enough, he'll just happen by and, oh my, yes, she would like to take a ride. As she climbs into the buggy, the flower of romance has begun to bud.

Now, for the most part, these romances are tame affairs. An evening's ride, maybe an ice cream or snack at a local restaurant. There's not many places, or too much reason, to spend a lot of money on a date. Maintaining the good reputation you grew up with and being a good conversationalist make more of an impression than a big bill for food you could have eaten at home. Nothing at all like city romances, where the young fellow comes to her house and ends up being the prize bull on exhibition. No, the Amish parents don't know who their offspring are out with, but they do trust them. After all, they are Amish.

Just being Amish isn't a guarantee of sainthood, though, especially when it comes to romantic endeavors. Living so close to the English world, if not in philosophy then at least in physical proximity, does tend to cause the young people to interact from time to time. With Amish girls being some of the most beautiful and the fellows the most handsome young men on earth, at least in their own opinion, it's inevitable that romance is just like ivy; it spreads across all boundaries these days.

I distinctly recall the third Saturday of last October in that respect, having gone down to town just after noon on a little business myself. It was a pleasant day, fall-cool and the like, as I tied up the hack by the courthouse. I had just knotted the rope when I happened to spy Ina standing across the square in the doorway to one of the stores.

Ina is Andy's youngest, the quiet one who does most of her talking with her dark brown eyes. I always held to the opinion she was a little too thin, needing to eat more, but her dad always thought me to the stupid side as well. Maybe it was just a hunch, but even from a distance I had the impression that Ina would have preferred I not see her. Her black bonnet had been replaced by a scarf, her jacket had a bit more fashion to it than what we see at church and I'd say the hem of that oh-so-Amish dress had been temporarily turned up an inch or two.

She looked real nice, being polite to anyone who strolled past and happened to nod to her, but I'm not going to say I approve of such carrying on. I'm just glad we don't have it as bad as some. It seems the closer our people get to the big city, the more what we know of as the dual personality tends to appear.

The fellow who comes our way selling power tools was the one who first tipped me off to this. He's from the Wooster area and, one Friday evening, decided to take his wife to some big hotel thereabouts for dinner. From what he said, they'd just finished and were paying the bill when he saw four or five very attractive Amish girls going into the ladies' room.

Paul figured he'd wait, him doing so much business with the Amish, and see if he knew some old friends. When the door opened again and the young ladies reappeared, he figured even if he did know them, he better hadn't admit it. Leather skirts, silk blouses and no sign of a prayer cap anywhere told him it was the girls' night out on the town.

Not wanting to be in that situation, I stuck close to the

side of the buildings as I strolled about my business. Fortunately for me, in just a minute a young fellow pulled up to the
curb in his automobile. To judge by the smile on her face, Ina
had an afternoon planned. As she started to get into the car,
her jacket parted to reveal she was wearing a most unusual
sweatshirt over her dress. All of a sudden everything fell into
place.

A fall Saturday means college football here in Ohio. Seeing as how Ina was wearing an Ohio State shirt and it was the
day of the big homecoming game, the next four hours were
well taken care of for her. Her brothers would be waiting for
Monday's paper for an account of the game while she, the sly
one, would play ignorant even though she'd seen it all.

Suzanna found herself in one of these interfaith relation-
ships, on the receiving end of the attention of a young Amishman, when she came to Holmes County on a college-based
tour of the area. Although she appeared quite normal and
seemed to be the average college girl, this group quickly discovered she had a problem. When they finally got the problem solved, I'd say all parties found what a small world it
really is.

Five weeks before this vanload of scholars went to
Holmes County, Suzanna had been living at home in Ger-
many. She had arrived in the United States just a few weeks
before as a foreign exchange student. Her sponsors, knowing
she had written a school paper on the peculiar Americans
called Amish, had signed her on for the trip.

That was all well and good, in theory at least, but then
the little problem set in. Suzanna could read and write English
very well. She could speak it, too, but not like Americans do
and certainly not as fast as city people do. The poor girl was
lost.

They all worried about Suzanna, trying their best to have

her keep pace until the second stop of the day. They'd just pulled into Mount Hope, up where they have the monthly horse sale, when one of the students on the trip came up with a plan. Suzanna spoke German and the Amish speak a dialect of the same. That vanload took a vote and decided Suzanna was going to find an Amish to talk to. If she didn't, they weren't going to let her back in the van.

Half believing this dire threat, Suzanna set off to the local hardware thinking that would be a good place to find some Amish. Being her lucky day, there was an Amish lady doing some shopping in there. Bringing up all her courage, the young lady struck up a conversation.

I can't speak for the rest of the world but, being Amish, the next best thing to discovering a long-lost relative is to find somebody from the old country. Even though the roots of the faith are in Switzerland, that's close enough. This Amish lady was so pleased to meet Suzanna that she just about talked the poor girl's ear off.

Somewhere in the midst of this conversation, the door to the store opened and in strolled the Amish lady's oldest son. He may be Plain, but he had an eye for a good-looking girl. In just a moment, he was in this conversation as well.

Time sort of slipped away in there that day. Before you knew it, it was time for Suzanna to rejoin her group and go on. I'd say there was some sadness in parting until the young fellow did a little quick thinking. He ambled over to the counter, got a piece of paper, a pencil and did some quick sketching.

"Now," he said, finishing off his map, "if . . . no, when you come back, this is how to find our farm. We would like you to come visit. If you do, I would like to give you a ride in my buggy."

With Momma Amish grinning the way she was, Suzanna

had no choice but to agree. Let us close this glimpse into the friendship by saying that Suzanna did come to visit, the young fellow did get a chance to show off his rig and . . . well, we'll just worry about that later.

Romance progresses by degree down in the Peoli Valley. It won't be long before you can count on a young couple to do their share of lap sitting, but we even do that backwards. Those aren't the world's tallest Amishmen you see driving a buggy down the road on a Saturday night. No, he's sitting on her lap as the hack trots down the open road. Come now, somebody's got to drive.

To be honest, I had my own problems a few years back when it came to romance. There was a very beautiful young lady who grew up well northwest of us, in Berlin. When she got to be twenty-five and not married, some began to worry about her. They thought she'd be a lot happier living around this area, a spot with our share of single men. Taking heed to all this advice, Mary found a place to live and a job not far from here.

It could be she was making her move before she got invited to any more of what the Amish call older-single-girls' outings. You might call it a spinsters' club, but that's neither here nor there. All that does matter is that I did take a shine to Mary, seeing all her noble qualities and having quite an eye for her.

The romance started off nice and slow, like it should. I didn't see Mary every day. Not every week, either. Actually I saw her only about once a month or so. After five years I was sure I was quite content, so happy that I was on the verge of asking her to marry me. Then, suddenly, she sent word through a mutual friend that she didn't care to see me again ever. Mary had discovered I'd told her a lie.

I feel bad about this, for lying is a sin. I feel worse, for

Mary is a fine Christian woman of virtue and I wouldn't want a moment's pain to come her way. There's something else that really makes me feel bad, though. I don't know which lie she caught me at.

Just within weeks of this most dark moment of my life, a bright spot appeared. It was that last warm day of fall that year as I happened to be strolling past Mill Pond. It was then that I remembered Our People aren't much for bathing suits. A lot of money for not much material. This came to mind as I happened to spot Sarah, Levi's oldest girl, out taking a swim.

Sarah is twenty-three now and not married, but it's not because of her looks. She's got that chestnut hair and light blue eyes of an absolute beauty. Sarah likes to stand up for herself, speak her own piece, and that scares the fellows. When I saw I had a chance to have a little fun on her, I seized the opportunity.

As quiet as I could, I slipped down to the water, tiptoed over, snatched up her clothes and made a run for it. Sarah saw what was happening, jumped out of the water and threw one of those big metal washtubs in front of her.

"Hey," she let out with a shout, stopping me in my tracks. She waited until I turned around and looked her right in the eye before she lit into me.

"I'd say you think you're smart, don't you, E. R.?"

"Could be," I answered back, "but I'd say you think there's a bottom in that tub, too."

No matter how it started, no matter how it's worked out, where these soon-to-be-marrieds are all headed is for one very special night. We do things old-fashioned back home. I can't tell you if any other congregation in the world still is like us, but it don't matter. What does matter is that a young couple has their lives in order with each other and their church. Everything is set as he lets her out of the buggy at her home

that evening. Nothing's said, but somehow it's been sensed.

The young lady will go to her room, but not to sleep. She's too busy listening for the sound of his buggy coming up

the lane. It is the first time he's done this and, when she hears those wheels, she starts intently watching her bedroom ceiling, looking for the beam of his flashlight.

It could be that if you'd do such a stunt in the city, you'd be arrested. Down in the Peoli Valley, he's just said, "Will you marry me?" When she comes downstairs, opens the door and they stay up all night making plans and finally meeting her parents, the answer is "Yes!"

Maybe it was just a hunch, but I was awake one night when Sis slipped in. It was just a few minutes later that I heard the wheels on the lane. I slipped over to the window, spied out and from the buggy jumped Junior Weaver.

Junior takes out his light, gets all set, aims it, pushes the button and nothing happens. Nothing. He hits it on the side of the buggy, pushes the button and there's nothing. He's just about ready to take the light apart when, all of a sudden, the front door opens downstairs and there's Dad.

Dad spied what was going on, jumped back into the house and shut the door. Now Junior's in a rush. He's shaking the light, spitting on the batteries, knocking the flashlight on the buggy, the dog starts barking, the rooster is crowing, the neighbor's lights are coming on and then the front door opens. Here's Dad. Real slowlike, Dad walks across the porch, down the steps and over to Junior. Dad reaches in his pocket and pulls out two flashlight batteries.

"Here," Dad says, handing Junior the batteries. "I suppose she could have done worse."

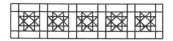 **6**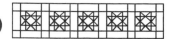

Work, Amish style

It's been a good, a great, year for the farmers around these parts. Plenty of rain, just enough sunshine and all the crops looking real good. As much as I've enjoyed driving nails for a living all these years, there's just something about the thought of turning the soil that gets me to smiling, even if those furrows are only in my mind.

One Amishman in three farms these days, but every man who goes to church in a buggy is a farmer in his heart. We're so crazy about farming that we all take some vacation time to work on the local threshing crews in July. Don't be thinking we'll be building many houses come October, either. We're on vacation again, helping bring in the corn. I'm getting used to this notion of one hundred forty-four stalks to the shock.

Working on a farm just feels good. It's like I'm in harmony with nature. Makes me tired, but feeling good when the sun goes down. Feel like I got something done that day. As great as that feeling is, though, it's nothing compared to the satisfaction we got when Junior Miller needed a barn.

57

It's been four summers now, back the year everything got so hot and dry. The heavy storms swept north up the valley that night, I remember. As welcome as the rain was, along with it came every farmer's nightmare—lightning. As the storm moved on, in its wake was that dull, orange afterglow that could only mean that somewhere a barn was on fire.

According to the story we heard, the bolt hit Junior's barn around one that Tuesday morning. In what seemed like just a minute, the whole place was in flames. Somehow they managed to save most of the livestock and some of the machinery. What with living out in the country and having a volunteer fire department, by the time help arrived what was once a barn was now just a pile of ash.

News of the calamity spread through the Amish world about as fast as that fire took down the barn. It was three days later, the next Friday morning in fact, when a fellow by the name of Jacob made his way to Junior's. For one entire day, Jake sat in the shade of the old oak tree and looked at the pile of rubble. He made no notes, had no sketches. All he did was look. When he stood up to go home at five that evening, word went out that Jake, boss carpenter and master barnbuilder, was ready for a barn raising.

Through word of mouth, letters, announcements in church and even an ad in a newspaper for the Amish called *The Budget,* news of the big event traveled. Tools were checked, muscles limbered up and a mass of people prepared to move in one direction, with one purpose, come one Saturday.

On the Thursday of raising week, a mason crew came in and laid the foundation. Supplies were carted in that evening and then sorted on Friday. On Saturday morning, as the sun started up around six-thirty, the buggies began rolling in. Soon cars and vanloads came bringing Amish and English alike from farther distances. At seven that morning, six hundred men were ready to work.

Jake was the boss this day. If he told you the beam was to be sixteen foot, then that's what it was. If he wanted you in the rafters, then that's where you worked. He was just like a circus ringmaster, directing a building project with the blueprint etched in his mind. It didn't matter if you were a farmer who had never hammered a thing or a master carpenter. You did what Jake told you, knowing he was right.

At noontime it was the women's turn to take charge for an hour. They spread a feast like you can't imagine. So much and so good it was like watching a magic show. Something was put on the table and it just disappeared. The ladies may not have driven too many nails but their contribution was appreciated.

By five that afternoon, the last buggy was headed for home. Where the ashes had been was now a barn one hundred twenty feet wide, one hundred fifty long and three stories high. Not only built, but roofed and whitewashed as well, ready for the evening's milking to be done. Some would call it a miracle, but it's just a fact of life around here.

There is no plaque marking the occasion, no sign of self-congratulations at the barn today. Junior did express his thanks in church and in the newspaper, but it wasn't necessary. It's just a part of being Amish, part of being family. Like a team of finely matched draft horses, the Plain People put aside their differences and pull together to help. There were a lot of tired muscles, but I'll tell you we can hardly wait to do it again.

Before you go to thinking that everything the Amish touch turns to gold, perhaps I should mention something. Sometimes those of the world get a real bargain in dealing with the Amish. Sometimes they get more than they bargained for, too.

Mr. Jones was getting along in years when he knew he needed another corncrib. He couldn't build it himself but, living on the northern edge of an Amish community, he figured he could find a carpenter or two. He put an ad in the local paper and, sure enough, the next day brought two young Amish carpenters to his door.

Yes, they could build the corncrib and the price was right. There were a few conditions, though. They could build the crib in two days if they could stay overnight. And they could stay overnight only if they brought their families.

Jones is no fool. He knew Ohio's Amish average seven children to a family, so he checked. There would be no problem as there were only six little ones between these two Amish. Ignoring his sixth sense, Mr. Jones struck the deal.

The next morning, near ten o'clock, the Amish families arrived and set to work. Work they did, hard work right up to suppertime. Yes, they would be delighted to share supper with the Jones family. One Amish wife thanked Mrs. Jones profusely and told her not to worry about breakfast, though, as they had brought some things for that. The carpenters put away their tools, got cleaned up and the adventure began.

The Amish sat down at the table, said their silent grace and proceeded to eat everything not nailed down. Not one slice of bread but six or seven. One fellow liked the cooking so much he ate a whole chicken. They weren't done until the table was completely bare.

Everyone retired to the living room and the Plain ones were very gracious guests. They made pleasant conversation, in between belches, and had a nice visit until eight o'clock. That was bedtime. They appreciated the Joneses' gesture of separate bedrooms, but it wasn't necessary. After all, they were family and off they went.

Somehow the room that was selected was that of the Jones family's oldest daughter, the one away at college. The room that has the stereo, which just happened to get turned on. Turned on to WMMS, rock-and-roll Cleveland, the volume up to eight notches out of ten and that's just where it stayed.

Well into evening, in between tunes on the radio, Mr. Jones heard a *bonk* coming from the Amish room, then another *bonk*. He tiptoed over and carefully opened the door to survey a most amazing scene.

The adults were stretched out on the floor, all snoring as loud as the radio. The children had found football helmets and baseball bats. The *bonk* was a bat connecting to a helmet. Mr. Jones put his finger to his lips and then made a sign to kill the radio. Without the music blaring, and with just the snoring now reverberating through the walls, he stumbled back to his own room.

You probably know how well the smell of bacon frying can carry. You can imagine that smell at five-thirty in the morning. That's what time the Amish ladies were up. At six-thirty the hammers were being swung outside. With no more chance of rest, Mr. and Mrs. Jones staggered out to watch the project come to a completion.

By eleven that morning a new corncrib was finished. The Amish loaded up, took their pay and, with smiles and handshakes all around, were off. The Joneses watched from the porch as the buggies went out the lane. With one final wave, the Amish turned onto the main road and were gone.

As the buggies disappeared into the distance, Mr. Jones turned to his wife and said, "You know, they did do a good job. The price was great. I was thinking, next year I may be needing a new barn . . ." History records that Mrs. Jones didn't talk to him for three solid weeks.

I got wind of this saga the last time I stopped by to get some harness repaired up the road. As meaningful as discussions can be down at the mill, when it comes to the exchanging of vital information, there's no place hereabouts that can compare to Valley Harness. From what I can tell, Little Stutzman's place is roughly equivalent to the English barbershop. It's the place for true insight, complete with commentary, on the rest of the world. Take, for example, why Japanese shoes are so cheap.

"I can tell you why," Stutzman was saying that first day I was in his shop to get some harness for the buggy replaced. "It's them boats. Those Japanese people send over great big boats to the San Francisco dock. There's a guy standing there, probably from Texas or Wyoming, who has a whole bundle of leather hides for sale.

"When those Japanese see all this good leather, they buy it all up and load it into their boat. Then they turn the boat around and head to Tokyo. The whole time they're floating across the Pacific, there's hundreds of Japanese people, all down in the hold, cutting up those hides and forming shoes.

"They're not near done when they get back to Tokyo, but that doesn't matter. They've got enough finished that they can load on all sorts of cardboard in the hold, too. They check their mail and then head right back toward San Francisco.

"About halfway across, all the shoes have been made. Those people put away their shoe tools and start folding cardboard into boxes. They've got it timed so well that they're slapping on the last label just as the boat's tying up to the dock. Then they start it all over again.

"That's why Japanese shoes are so cheap. You can't get people to work like that in this country."

I don't want to burst Little Stutzman's bubble, but I don't think the Japanese work like that. There's no sense in arguing, though. That's what he's heard and now repeated a thousand times over. Around Valley Harness, that's all it takes to constitute fact. I'm just glad Stutzman makes harness and doesn't write for the newspaper. Although, given some things I've read, maybe he does.

The Amish have no problem with working hard. It's sort of hoped that should you die in the cause of laboring, it might give you a leg up on salvation. Nothing for certain, for that is vain and we do strive to avoid vanity, but it might help. Hard work sets a good example for the young and old alike and even for the outsider now and then.

A long time ago, long before me, there was an Amish family that took in a foster boy. Once in a while the Plain People do that, not to add another member to the faith, but because children need a good home. A good home is just what this family gave Jack. They cared for him and taught him to love his work. It was with more than a little regret when Jack turned eighteen and went off to make his own way in the world.

It wasn't long before Jack settled down in Indiana and had a family of his own. Jack always fondly recalled his Berlin family of Amish, though, even as things turned bad at home. Bad they were, for Jack's boy, John, was a real troublemaker.

John never could stay out of trouble for very long. Stole some things as a boy and got sent to the Navy as punishment. Deserted that and raised all sorts of heartache not only in Indiana but Illinois and Ohio, too. Oh, did he have a real fracas in Lima, up in the northwest part of the state one time. But for all the problems he caused, John never once made trouble in Berlin.

Some say it was because there's nothing in Berlin that John never came that way. Could be, though, that John always remembered what his father had said about the Amish. How he respected them and how they treated him with respect, too. The more you think about it. could be it was respect for Amish principles that kept Jack's boy from raising Cain down home. For whatever reason, the Plain People never had to deal with Jack's boy, John Dillinger.

 **7**

Recreation

Thinking that the Amish are hopelessly addicted to work just might be the greatest mistake somebody could make about the Plain People. Work has its place, but among us a busy schedule is never too full not to allow room for a little fun. An Amish definition of fun might differ dramatically from the English, however.

To start to get a handle on true fun, the Amish don't have to go any farther than right around the house. There's not one single family I know of that doesn't love to spend time together. From great-grandpa right down the line to the newborn, the generations blend together when excitement's in the wind.

There's games to be played, trampolines to bounce on and nature walks to take. Jake's bunch loves the softball, Andy's crowd is big on the volleyball and Levi's got quite a co-ed basketball squad most evenings. No matter the activity, the whole family enjoys.

Beyond the physical fun, just about every family in these parts enjoys exercising the mind, too. Pretty much every evening is spent reading the Bible, Luther's translation in a Gothic script, and sharing favorite stories from that wonderful text. If that's not enough to inspire a man, then there's a book we all enjoy called the *Martyr's Mirror*. That's the one where the terrible sufferings of our ancestors, some of whom died for their love of Christ, have been recorded. It makes one glad to be alive and grateful to those who gave so much for the right to be different.

The Amish save most of their reading energies for that newspaper I mentioned, *The Budget*. It's a grand paper, coming out once a week from Sugarcreek. It is so good that the paper has inspired a recycling movement down at the local mill.

Levi and Andy, brothers-in-law that have been here since time began, run the mill and they've got a company subscription for the paper. All us trustees of the valley, the ones the women insist on calling the loafers, know what time the mail comes to the mill. Anytime after that is likely to find us moseying down that way. It's a real ritual these days, making sure the paper gets read.

Levi will get the mail, open up the paper and read all the big block ads. Then he folds it up and puts it in the trash. Andy will go over, pull the paper out of the can and then peruse the classifieds. When he's all done, he folds it up and back into the can it goes.

About the time the paper hits the bottom of the trash bin, Ammon is up off the bench and headed for it. He'll pull out the first section, the one with the auction announcements, and read those. Back in the trash it goes so Lester can get up and pull out the section that has news from Pennsylvania congregations. It is such a great newspaper that on and on this goes until we all get to read our favorite part. Then on Friday we tell each other what we've read.

If it does seem foolish to you that grown men would go through such a ritual, you aren't alone. The thought did cross my mind, too, but it only took once to learn.

It was the first Thursday I had been in the trustees. I saw Levi look through the paper and put it in the can. Natural as could be, I said, "Hey, why don't you pass that over here?"

Natural as could be, Levi said, "Why don't you spend sixty cents and buy your own?"

Given a choice between spending sixty cents and trash picking, I'll keep recycling if you don't mind.

Some say it wasn't too long after the Amish broke away from the Mennonites in 1693 that the Plain People discovered something unique about the human body. They found each

one of them had a mouth and with that mouth they could speak words. With those words they formed first sentences and then whole paragraphs. It has progressed to the point today that whenever two or more Amish gather together, good talk breaks out.

The Amish love to visit, more fun than even reading. Visit family, visit friends, just visit and share the time. Maybe it's getting to be a lost art among the city crowd, but it's to the point of perfection among the buggy crowd. If you really want some good talk, maybe you'd just better investigate what's known as a horse auction.

The second Saturday of every month finds the barn in Mount Hope, up in Holmes County, packed with the fellows. Those are good sales, but we generally save our energies for the big sale of the year in Columbus. It comes the first Tuesday and Wednesday of February each year. How big? How about seven hundred head of draft horses and six thousand people, most in the black felt hats and bonnets. It's a real spectacular that was more spectacular than usual a couple of years back.

The sale had slowed down that Tuesday afternoon so a few of us went out for a stroll around the fairgrounds. We noticed a lot of city folk going into another building close by and thought we'd investigate. We wandered along the back of the building, jiggling doors, and sure enough, one was open. As it was open, we just made our way into something called a Vacation and Travel Show.

To say it was interesting would be an understatement, what with hundreds of exhibitors and all sorts of free stuff to pick up, but it was no horse sale. We'd seen just about everything we cared to look at when up steps a policeman. A real policeman.

He nodded and wondered if he could help us. We appreciated his gesture, but it wasn't necessary. We could take care of ourselves, thank you. Then he wondered how each of us had gotten in. When he heard we came in the unlocked back door, he figured we ought to go back out that same direction. That or pay the $4.50 admission at the front gate. It should go without saying that out the door we went.

To this day my associates are mystified as to how that policeman was so clever. There were more than a thousand people in that travel show crowd looking at power boats, recreational vehicles and cruise brochures. The fellows don't see how he knew we were the only ones who didn't pay.

I'm not going to say, but I think I've got a clue. Indeed, there were a thousand in the throng. Perhaps it had something to do with the fact that of the thousand, there was only six of us with the black felt hats, beards but no mustaches and five-button pants. Something about standing out, I'd say.

Women are not exempt from sale excitement, either, I might note. They may not care for the horses like I do, but put the pretty quilts up on the block and you'd better stand back. This I know firsthand.

We were going to have an auction to raise money for Valley Ridge School. Someone announced they were going to start selling the hand-stitched quilts in fifteen minutes. It was my misfortune to be standing along the line between the food tent and the sale ring. I didn't end up in plaster but it did take two full weeks for all the bruises and trample marks to heal.

One time back, some English friends took us down to a sale well southwest of us. The sale bill looked real good and I'd say we were pretty excited about it. Once we got there and looked over the goods, we had our eye on several items that just might come in at a bargain price.

The problem came when I went to register to bid. I forgot I wasn't in an Amish community for this sale. Around here you just tell them your name. A man's word goes a long way. Down at this sale things tended to run a little different. A little more English.

Real patientlike, I waited my turn to get a number to bid. The young lady who was cashiering must not of been having a good day is all I can figure. She was sort of snippy asking to see my driver's license.

I looked at her kind of stupid, thinking she must be kidding with me, and told her I didn't have such as that. Then she wanted to see a credit card. I'll tell you, I go for those less than a driver's license. She seemed real ticked off and asked for my Social Security card. When I told her, being self-employed, the government says I'm exempt from that, she laid down her own brand of the law.

"Well, you can't bid," she snapped. "Next."

I shrugged my shoulders, dumbfounded that our great society no longer accepts greenbacks. Figuring that was it, I started to leave when I heard the fellow behind me let out with a string of words I don't care to use. "If you can't trust those guys, who can you?" was all I can repeat of his saying.

The cashier was insistent: no identification meant no number. This fellow dressed in coveralls and old work boots gave her a look, didn't say any more and marched right out the door. Not wanting to make trouble, I headed out that way myself. I'd no more gotten out the door when here came this fellow back, now with the auctioneer in tow.

That auctioneer took one look and told me to come along inside. Back we went, bucking to the head of the line. It was short and sweet, the auctioneer saying, "Register him."

The young lady started to argue, but it got cut real short. I don't recall the exact words, but it was something about cashiers being a dime a dozen. I felt bad, real bad, about the trouble but the two fellows wouldn't have none of it.

"Forget it," the auctioneer said. "I need business from you guys."

The other fellow, once he got over his mad, cooled down and was real pleasant. I was so grateful for him standing up for me, a total stranger, that I gave him one of our business cards and told him I hoped to return the favor. He seemed grateful in return, giving me one of his cards.

I've got no reason to doubt the printing on the card, especially after seeing the way some talked to this new friend of mine. Funny, though, if you're smart enough to cashier a sale, you'd think you'd be smart enough to recognize your county commissioner, too.

There's one kind of sale that has priority over any horse or quilt auction. When a family or an individual has racked up the hospital bills, that's something we don't waste any time doing something about. I'd suppose the idea is sort of like a barn raising: somewhere there's somebody in need and it's time to lend a hand.

You see, the Amish don't live by insurance. They live by the assurance of their community, the assurance that a friend and neighbor will always be there when you need, but sometimes even that isn't enough. Sometimes you've got to be reminded how much some care.

Sarah is a fine woman, a tower of strength in her congregation. It hurt everyone when she took sick. It hurt even more when it was found that she would need a liver transplant, and right now, to survive. They were willing and able at the hospital to do the operation right then and sure enough, Sarah pulled through quite well. When her recovery was assured, the hospital people were kind enough to pass on a bill for a quarter of a million dollars. They were good about it, though; they only required payment in the next sixty days.

When word spread of such city generosity, the community took over. A charity auction was organized for one Saturday. With news spreading throughout Amish country, the idea was to try to retire as much of that debt as possible. For many days, all Sarah and her family could do was wait and hope for the best.

It came that Saturday and the auctioneer started his chant at nine. All proceeds, even the food concessions, were going to Sarah's cause. The people kept coming, they kept bidding and they kept buying. The hammer fell for the last time at eight that evening. When the accounting was done, I heard tell the sum of three hundred thousand dollars had been collected. It felt real good to be a human being that day.

As remarkable as this bit of charity is, this sale will always be remembered by the crowd hereabouts as my coming-out party. Thanks to a quirk of fate and some very fast thinking, I was finally recognized for the talents I have developed over the years. In the blink of an eye, I was proclaimed Community Storyteller, source of an evening's entertainment and imparter of wisdom. From my side of the fence, all I was doing was trying to stay alive.

Several of us had come up from Peoli to Sarah's sale, more to do visiting than anything else. We were standing off in the yard, talking and telling some jokes for most of the day. We'd been clowning around for some time when an older fellow made his way over and joined in the community circle.

One thing led to another and before too long this fellow was a part of the conversation as well. He seemed quite interested we were from the Peoli area. He'd never been there, but had heard some about it. Seems he had a daughter living and working not far from there for a while.

He introduced himself as Jonas Miller. Trying to fight a hunch, I found myself asking if he was the Jonas from Sugarcreek or the one from near Berlin.

"Oh, Berlin," he says. "Do you know the place?"

I admitted I'd been there a few times but didn't know much about the area. Then this Jonas launched into his family tree, wondering if I knew this son of his or that. Maybe there was one or two or seven of them that I'd heard of, but I kept playing coy. Then he went through his daughters, all five of them, ending up with the baby of the family, Mary. This Mary was the one who had lived down near Peoli for several years, in fact.

"You know," Jonas went on, "we heard Mary was seeing a fellow while she lived down there. From what we know, his name is E. R. Beachy and he's a no-account."

I nodded along because I'd heard the exact same thing about him, too. I didn't need eyes in the back of my head to know all my associates were looking at me. I didn't need to be a mind reader to tell you what was being thought, either. That wasn't my concern right then. All of a sudden my only concern was surviving to another sunset.

On and on Jonas went, how he was a man of peace but he wouldn't be accountable for his actions if he ever met this Beachy fellow. How he could forgive, but his temper would get the better of him, for Beachy had pushed him right to the limit.

"Say," this elderly Jonas said to me out of the blue, "I didn't get your name."

"It's Mose Yoder," I said back, not blinking an eye.

It wasn't too long after that when our driver was ready to head for home. We all said our good-byes, piled in the van and were off. I sat in the first row of seats, thanking my lucky stars in one thought and wondering if anybody was going to say anything in the next. We must have gone thirty miles toward home before the axe fell.

"Hey, E. R.," Andy said from the seat behind me, "you know that telling a lie is a sin?"

"Yep."

"Hey, E. R., you know that Jonas Mary?"

"Yep."

"Hey, E. R., you that guy he was talking about?"

"Yep."

"Hey, E. R., you're not half as dumb as I thought."

"Nope."

As that van rolled toward home, I found myself recounting one story after another for the enjoyment of the loafers. As I wove a thin thread of truth through each saga, I knew I had become a man of respect, admired for my creativity as well as my storytelling ability. Until my dying day, I will be remembered as the man who, while sparring on the edge of disaster with an angry father, thought fast enough to live to tell another story.

Yes, I fibbed my name was Mose Yoder. Yes, I'd fibbed a time or two or twenty to Mary. All things considered, I can't make the promise I'll never fib again. After all, if Jonas ever figures out . . . Well, it's not a pretty sight, seeing a man dragged down the road behind a buggy. Not saying that he would, but I'm not going to take no chances, neither.

All this fun I've been speaking of involves groups of people, sometimes large groups, socializing under the pretext of business. To us that's fun, a common way to enjoy each other's company. It is just as common, though, for some to have a little fun at the expense of their friends. That's all well and good, unless you happen to be the friend.

I have reached the conclusion that Amish women are very happy as wives and mothers. Being so happy, they figure that all their unmarried friends must be unhappy. It is therefore the duty of these married ladies to cure this misery. You might call it matchmaking but we know it as propping up.

Now I'm not going to name any names, but Freeman and Mary are good friends of mine up in Holmes County. Good

enough friends that I was invited to their family reunion five years ago last July.

I have no problem with such gatherings for they reflect a favorite hobby of mine, genealogy. Like all the Plain People, we've got quite a chart showing our pedigree. I had no problem in accepting this invitation, either, even though hindsight proved something different.

On that Saturday, bright and early, I got a ride up to Freeman's. We visited a bit over coffee, got the buggy hitched up and off we all went. Belle, Freeman's buggy horse, isn't the fastest thing these days so it took about an hour to cover the five miles to the park.

Once we got to the reunion, Amish social order took over. Freeman's boys took care of parking the horse and buggy. Mary and the girls took care of the food. Freeman and I joined all the other fellows, sitting and talking.

After about half an hour, it was the women's turn to come

over and check me out. The first thing one said was, "Why didn't you bring your wife and children?"

When I told her I wasn't married, she said, "Oh, how strange."

I happened to glance at Mary, who was blushing, but it didn't bother me. It didn't bother me for about ten minutes, not until Freeman let out with, "Oh, look, here comes our friend and neighbor, Widow Miller."

Sure enough, here comes a thirty-year-old or so lady across the way, toting her picnic basket. She makes a line right for Freeman's table, puts the basket down right across from me and says, "It's nice to meet you, E. R. Freemans have told me all about you."

I said, "That's very nice. They didn't say a word about you."

About two weeks later I was reminded of what a pleasant day that was. In the margin of a letter from Freeman, in very delicate handwriting, was, "We always enjoy reading your letters. We are sure there are others who would like to hear from you as well."

That was no big thing for I was going to Freeman's for a visit the next weekend. After a Saturday morning of helping the boys in the field, I wasn't amazed to see an extra buggy at Freeman's hitching post. What a surprise it wasn't to go into the house and extend my greetings.

It was a pleasant dinnertime there and, after a little visiting, I was kind enough to ride with Arlene Miller back to her home. I was back to Freeman's within twenty minutes, long before he expected me, but Mary already had this one figured out.

Just before supper, I thought it best to put on my Sunday clothes. About halfway through the meal I mentioned that I thought I'd go out for a walk that evening.

"Great," chimed Freeman. "I'll go with you. That way I can show you where all these people you met at the reunion live."

There was a great, long silence and then the distinct sound of Mary's shoe connecting to Freeman's shin. She scowled at him and then smiled at me. Scowled at him, smiled at me. Finally the big ox realized he'd better stay home and fix the window before it broke.

Sure enough, at a crossroads just out of sight from both houses, there was a buggy waiting. As I reflect on all the fun the Amish can have, I'd suppose that next six months of my life did have some enjoyment. I wonder if Arlene found me interesting or if she considered me the ultimate challenge. Nothing needs changing more than a contented bachelor.

I chewed tobacco, I smoked my pipe, I drank coffee by the gallon, my clothes were held together by safety pins and dental floss, I did what I pleased and I was happy before I met Arlene. I was so happy she set to immediately reforming me. For six months I was in misery, sneaking a smoke here and begging for coffee on the sly there.

I suffered but not in vain. I kept introducing Arlene to other bachelors and telling what a noble woman she was. For two years I searched, long after our romance had cooled to being no more than speaking acquaintance. Finally that perfect male was found and a new adventure began.

I was quite pleased to be invited to the wedding not as a participant but as a guest. I wished them both well as I spit tobacco juice and took a puff on my pipe. I would of liked to stay longer, the coffee being so good, but I had to get on home. I'd bought some new fishing line to sew up the seam of my pants with and wanted to get to that before dark. At least I was reasonably confident they'd be happy as I pulled out of the wedding and headed for home. I knew I sure was.

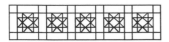 **8**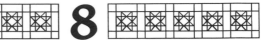

The neighborhood

I saw Woody Hershberger the other day. That probably doesn't mean anything to you, but Woody is a living legend around here. Woody's not his real name, but none of us would have been real keen on being called whatever it was his parents named him. I don't actually recall the name myself, only Woody, that name we all gave him. What is real, though, is Woody's claim to immortality.

It's been thirty years at least now since Woody decided he was going to have the world's fastest bicycle. Woody went out and got himself in good physical shape first and then set to work on the bicycle itself. To achieve all this speed he wanted, Woody knew he had to make the cycle lighter. Therefore the first thing he took off was the brakes.

I never said Woody was smart, only he was going to have the world's fastest bicycle, but it went downhill from there. Literally downhill, right to the bottom of the steepest decline in the county, on Valley Ridge Road. When Ervin and I got

there on our bikes to witness the event, Woody was just starting down the hill.

Credit must be given to Woody, for neither Ervin nor I
had ever seen anybody ride that fast before. He was going a
blue streak. About the time we up top really appreciated how
fast he was going, Woody was beginning to realize the first of
two problems.

You see, when you come to the bottom of Valley Ridge
Road, you have to turn. It's either left or right onto Valley
Road, but not straight. Not yet at least. About the time Woody
realized he'd have to make a decision, he caught sight of the
second problem. The entire foot of that decline was covered
with gravel. Whichever way he went, he was assured of a fall
and at least a broken bone or two.

Much to our surprise, the inventive Woody created a third
option when he came to the bottom of the hill. He went
straight. Straight into the concrete bridge on the far side of the
road.

To this day, I can still see that bike stop dead and Woody
doing a perfect one-and-a-half somersault into the creek. He
no more than hit the water than we saw a fishing pole fly up
in the air, heard Willie Troyer scream and let out running.

Ervin and I rushed down to the bridge in terror, sure that
the end had come for Woody and reforming our wicked ways
the whole way down. We didn't have any wicked ways back
then, but that didn't keep us from reforming anyway. Troyer
was still running, out of sight by now. As we reached the bottom
of the hill and looked over the railing, there lay Woody right
beside Willie's tackle box. He had a glazed-over look to his
eyes, having must of missed Willie by no more than a foot
when he came flying in from outer space.

Being but ten years old, I'd say we handled the emergency quite well. Ervin and I dragged Woody out of the creek,

laid him over the frame of his bicycle—him dangling there like he was a deceased Indian from a century ago strapped across a pony—and walked him home. We dumped him at his back door, knocked twice and then ran like Willie Troyer to get away before Mrs. Hershberger got there.

Woody recovered his health, but he never was the same. When he got to be of age, he ended up marrying one of those Swartzentruber Amish girls. That was fifteen children ago and she's expecting again. He'd probably have that glazed look in his eyes even if he wouldn't of gone over the bridge, all things considered.

Woody lives just over the ridge from our place, back by the big oak and next farm south of Ammon's. Maybe they've got a different kind of water coming out of the wells down there, come to think on it. Being creative and all, Woody has his unusual traits, but then again Ammon does, too. I'd say Ammon has got saving money down to a science.

Every day of his life, saving money has always been a high-priority item for Ammon. I'm not saying he's as cheap as Old Miller, that fellow I mentioned earlier with an urge to be giving the wife a shot now and then, but Ammon does tend to be frugal. It seems like he was always running off to the store to buy something on sale, whether he needed it or not. From there he's usually off to the bank, putting all those nickels and dimes away.

That's all well and good, Ammon certainly not wasting any gasoline on these jaunts, but several of us did comment on his means of transportation. That old standardbred mare of his, now pushing thirty-five, couldn't be making too many more miles with that buggy behind her. Andy claimed he'd seen the horse had one of those senior-citizen discount cards for herself, but I don't think that's so. Ammon always figured there was one more mile left in that chestnut mare, so it was no worry to him. No worry at least until that one day we all remember so well.

The best addition to the banking industry has to be the drive-through windows. Don't have to hunt for a parking place anymore, just pull right in line and take care of business. Of course, it being Friday, Ammon was in line with everybody who just got paid down at the pottery. Four or five cars, a buggy and then a whole long string of automobiles all the way out into the street. Everybody rushing, wanting to get a little spending money over the lunch hour.

The line moves along and it comes Ammon's turn. He no sooner finished his transaction when that buggy horse of his let out with a shudder and proceeded to die right there in the drive-through. Some say it was heart attack, but I don't know that matters. A long line of cars behind, a dead horse in front, and Ammon sitting there trying to make like there was nothing out of the ordinary going on until he figured out what to do next. I'd say there were several more candidates for heart failure right about then. Nobody had ever had a horse die at the bank before.

Everybody rushed around awhile, wondering what to do, before somebody thought to go across the street to the gas station. They've got a wreck truck there and, sure enough, they were happy to lend a hand. They weren't going to haul the horse to the local rendering plant, but they would clear the lane at least.

All this excitement happened around noontime as the bank president was having his lunch down at the Lamplight Inn. He came strolling up the street about one, just like he always does. He might have noticed the buggy parked in his lot. He probably noticed Ammon, sitting under the maple tree waiting for the truck from the rendering plant. One thing for sure, judging by the way he ripped and tore there for a while, he did notice a dead horse laying in the bank's front yard.

It really didn't bother Ammon since the carcass truck would be along soon. It sure didn't bother the gas station people, either, I'd say, being as they were a payment or two behind to the bank anyway. It sure did upset that bank president, though. Some say he was shouting he wasn't going to allow no more buggies in the bank and other thoughtless comments. Fortunately his assistant got out a folder or two to remind the boss of a few things. Something about the Plain People deposits at that bank totaling not tens but hundreds of thousands. Just like that, all that anger was gone from Mr. Bank President. Reminded of the value of a dollar, the bank's leader was soon seen outside with his arm around Ammon's shoulders, regretting the unfortunate death and wondering if Ammon had ever considered the possibility of financing his next four-footed purchase. Ah, the things we do for money.

It's the next place southwest to Ammon's where the Amishness tends to get a little primitive. That's the other bunch of the area, the conservative crowd, the ones who somehow figure indoor plumbing to be sinful.

It must of been fate that led me along that backroad the first week of November last year. Considering the time of year, the weather was fairly pleasant. It was a good thing, the sun shining and all, this good weather allowing me to savor an absolute circus at Mahlon's farm.

It wasn't Ringling Brothers' three-ring tent, but people probably would of paid to have seen an act like this one. It would be far too simple to just say the clowns in this show were hillbillies, writing it off to their peculiarities. No, this one was a spectacular to be savored and it needs told.

All summer long I'd seen signs by the road that Mahlon was selling produce, homegrown vegetables. He was advertising pretty heavy, signs out by the big road and all, trying to draw traffic down his way. I'd been by once and seen he'd even built a shed, a twenty-foot-square little house, to sell his goods right by the side of the road in front of the home place. As I trotted past this November morning, much to my surprise, the shed was gone.

I slowed up and appraised the situation. From ruts in the mud I could tell this fellow had taken his team of big, black Percheron draft horses and hitched them to this shed. He'd dragged it from the side of the road recently, maybe even that morning, through the yard and around behind the barn. I followed the tracks till they stopped, looked up and saw that he had the shed stuck on a dirt mound maybe four feet high. This fellow, his wife, the eleven children and the four horses were pulling with all their might trying to get the shed unstuck. I could tell they had a problem. I could also tell, with the exception of the old man, everybody including the horses was mad about something. Furious, neck-vein-bulging mad, in fact, and when I got to the bottom of the problem, I could see why.

Every year old Mahlon likes to grow melons to sell. He uses this shed as a roadside stand. Every April he drags it from by the barn to the roadside and hangs out a shingle. Every November he drags it back, through the yard, around the barn and, for the past six years, he's gotten it stuck on the same dirt mound.

Mahlon was absolutely dumbfounded when I asked him why they didn't level off the dirt mound before the dragging began the next time. It was an idea that had never occurred to him. Obviously the thought had dawned on the rest of the family, not to mention the horses. I could feel their blood pressures, already at the boiling point, just about ready to turn to steam.

It was an ideal time to be moving on, before any more great revelations came my way. I wound my way on home, chuckling the whole way. By the time I made it through our back door, I was absolutely hysterical in laughter.

I was still laughing about this clown when I stopped over to see Mervin for a few minutes. That Mahlon fellow is really something and I'm glad I don't have too much to do with him. I figured Mervin would appreciate it, him doing some business with that family from time to time.

Appreciate it he did, getting some chuckle out of my account of the exploit. When I got all done, he laughed and went over to his bookcase and pulled out a paperback book called *Die Calendar*.

Die Calendar is really our almanac. It's got that zodiac mumbo jumbo and the witty sayings, but more, too. There's an outline in there for each month's church services, reminding us what Scriptures will be read and hymns sung. That's all well and good, but it was the last section that Mervin found most interesting.

That's the pages that list out the bishops, preachers and deacons for congregations across the country. Mervin thumbed through until he found the right page. He ran his finger along the print until he found what he wanted. Giving me a sickening grin, he motioned for me to take a look at what he found.

I said I don't like those people and don't want anything to do with them. I don't know much about them and, until that moment, could have cared less. Even without looking at the print, somehow I knew what was coming.

The one called Mahlon? Among that crowd they call him Bishop Mahlon. He's the head man. Ah well, if he's the smartest one of them all, that says something about the rest of the bunch. I'll tell you this, though. Those size sevens of mine are getting real comfortable in my mouth these days.

From time to time, some strangers to the area will rave about how beautiful Amish women of this neck of the woods tend to be. I cannot argue that fact, holding to the opinion my wife is the most beautiful girl in the world and all the rest of the community finished in a tie for second place. I don't give it much thought, Peoli Valley not exactly having an annual beauty contest or the like. Still, some come looking for that secret of beauty and, just for those curious ones, I investigated and believe I have found that secret Amish recipe.

First would be to rise around five-thirty in the morning to be firing up the stove. While the potatoes are beginning to fry, get the washing machine to be thinking on its first load of laundry for the day. By six-thirty, when the man of the house has eaten and gotten off to work, then the lady can really indulge in the beauty tricks.

Take that first load of laundry out of the tub and replace it with the second load. Then hang the first load, still wet from the wash, out on a line between the house and the big maple out back. The trick here is, as soon as that wash is hung out, to grab ahold of a hoe and get into the garden to start thinning out the weeds.

The beauty treatment continues right through a hanging out of the second load of wash and a quick lunch. Then carefully harness the buggy horse, attach the shafts to the rigging and head over to the neighbors for putting in a quilt. Three hours there of vigorously exercising both fingers and gums does wonders for the body.

By this time, as the sun begins to decline, it's back to home. Take in the wash, folding some and making another pile to be pressed in another basket. Be sure to get a huge

supper on the stove, timed to be ready to eat within a minute of when the husband comes home from work.

Being such a comprehensive beauty treatment, it can't be too surprising to learn the remedy continues after supper. Be sure to wash the dishes spotless and then get the ironing done. With a touch of luck, there's just enough time to get a few chapters read in the Good Book before it's time to put out the light and curl into bed.

Not what the average beauty book tells you? That could

B.C.

be, but I've never read one anyway. I'll stand by my earlier statement, though. That's the way she spent the day and Mrs. Beachy, the girl of my dreams, is now and always will be beautiful.

There's another kind of beauty around these parts, worth a little more to me than that physical side so many find important. Around here there's an inner glow, something I never could describe or bottle up. It just happens and sometimes it gets hard to explain.

About five miles northwest of here is a Mennonite church. They're our cousins, not in terms of blood but in the faith. The Amish are the more conservative offshoot of the religious heritage, but there's a lot more to it than that.

If the notion of different factions of the Amish tends to confuse, then the study of the Mennonites would absolutely dumbfound. There's fourteen different conferences, or governing bodies, of Mennonites in Ohio today. Then there's the Conservative Mennonites, conference members or independents. There's also Amish Mennonites, also called Beachy Amish, floating around. Throw in the horse-and-buggy Old Order Mennonites and then the house Mennonites, the ones worshipping in the home and not a church, and this is one real jumble.

That's just Ohio by the way. There's different kinds of Amish and Mennonites in Pennsylvania, Indiana, Wisconsin, Texas, Montana, and a whole lot of other places we've heard of but know little about. How people can say all the Amish do this or Mennonites do that is a mystery to me. Maybe someday some of those smart English will be able to explain it. Our People sure can't.

Just like with the Amish, all these folks operate under the same Scripture, the same basic belief as any other Protestant faith. It's in the interpretation of the faith where all the differences show up. Some Mennonite women don't wear prayer caps while other factions look downright Amish except they drive cars.

Some scholars use the car as that signifying break between Mennonite and Amish. Others point to education, citing that most of the Mennonites support higher learning while we limit ourselves to the basic school of eight grades. Still others use electricity as the determinant. Certainly each standard has its merits to help in understanding, but around here we might be on to something even more identifying about the Mennonites.

Don's a feed salesman that stops in at the mill about once a month or so. He belongs to that Mennonite church in our end of the country. For a young fellow, he's pretty smart, being well versed on both Mennonites in general and that particular congregation's life histories.

Often times, especially in Holmes and Wayne counties, Mennonite churches have a large percentage of former Amish in their membership. That's not the case with our neighbors, not a single one born Amish on the roster. As a matter of fact, from what Don told us, more than half the church had converted from another faith to being Mennonite. Even the pastor had started out a Lutheran before coming over.

Around here, we see that mission of evangelism as the real dividing line between the Amish and the Mennonites. With representatives like Don, their church is spreading the good word wherever they can find a listener. The Mennonites witness, testify, missionary and just plain evangelize around the world. They're growing in this country real steady and spreading like wildfire in what some call the developing countries, wherever that might be.

Don was pretty serious with us all at the mill when he was in, telling each of us we should be spreading the Word. I was sitting there on the sacks of dog food listening until he got just about finished. Then I said, "I'm not much for being the evangelist, Don."

"Oh yes, you most certainly are, E. R.," he said, turning to face me. "You're an evangelist even if you don't know it. You evangelize with your appearance, your buggy and by being a people apart. You evangelize, yes you do."

I shook my head and said, "No, Don, I'm not an evangelist. I'm an example." I heard Andy muttering something about liking to make an example out of me, but I didn't pay no attention. Instead I let that sink in for a minute before I went on.

"Do you know I, personally, don't believe in God, Don?"

His eyes bulged out in shock at such a heathen remark, but I held my hand up to hold the floor.

"I don't believe," I went on, "because I know. I can see the Lord in every blade of grass, every sunrise, every rainstorm, every single thing. That's a contented feeling.

"It's contentment, too, to know there's others feeling just like I do. Not only feeling like me, but willing to be there should anyone, anyone, need a hand. We trust each other enough to depend on them, and there's not too much else you can ask of a man.

"There's a contentment in living my life, the only life I've ever known, the way I'm comfortable with. Living in peace, you don't have to be wrong for me to be right. I don't force anything on you and you give me the same privilege. That's a good feeling, too.

"I don't force my life on anyone but, should they ask about what they see, I'll answer. Some do, and one question leads to another. Once in a while, enough questions and one of the world becomes one of Our People. Rare, but it happens. A life one with nature, one with peace, one with man and one with our Lord, all for the asking. Few do, but maybe those are the ones prepared to hear the answers."

It was quiet for a bit in the mill that day. You could tell Don was thinking of all the arguments he could toss back. You could also see him rejecting each as soon as he thought of it. It took a minute or two before a twinkle came to his eyes.

"E. R., you ever get tired of riding around in a buggy, the Mennonites sure could use a persuasive preacher like you."

I twinkled right back as I said, "You ever get tired of that electricity, I'll be right here waiting for you."

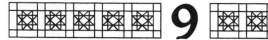 **9**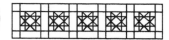

The English

Yes sir, all things considered, this is one pretty nice neighbor-hood, even with old Mahlon down the way. I'd say every one of us counts his lucky stars we don't have to face the plague of Holmes and Wayne counties. Four million sightings last year alone of that bird called the Rubber-Necked Arm Flinger or, by its more common name, an English tourist.

It's given most of us cause to think. Amish people have been Ohioans since 1809, but tourists have been flocking to the Plain People for only ten years or so. It's too bad when those strangers come looking that they don't find any Amish. More and more every day Ohio turns into another Lancaster County, Pennsylvania. A whole lot of people forget tourism and pitch commercialism, forgetting principles and promoting profit. A few make a lot at the expense of many. Anymore, it just don't seem fair.

If you think I'm off base on this issue, maybe you'd better take a look at some counties' tourist information. Last time I looked at one, of the nearly one hundred places listed, less than ten were Amish owned and they were claiming that was "Amish Country." You can be assured that the housewife, the farmer, the carpenter and the mason who happen to be Amish and can't even get to town for business on Saturday anymore appreciate it less than I do. When we talk about the damage those big tour buses do to roadways or the dumb, intrusive questions some folks ask, it's a good thing the Amish are a peaceful, patient people.

Maybe it all comes down to the fact the Amish don't have some sort of public-relations fellow spreading the news. Somebody hears, or somebody says, and the next thing you know is that it's a fact. Sometimes English people tell us things we never heard of, we never even dreamed of, that are supposed to be really Amish.

Four or five of us were down at Ammon's the other day, standing there watching him paint his gate blue. We were pretending we were state workers, I guess. It was right in the middle of the afternoon when up the road comes a car.

The best thing the state of Ohio ever did was put county stickers on the license plates of automobiles. Now you can spot a stranger right away. This car was from the Cleveland area and Jake says they don't get no stranger than that. At any rate, the fellow driving the car looks over, jams on the brakes, jumps out and runs over.

"Is it true?" he asks.

"Could be," I replied. "What?"

"I heard that when an Amishman paints his gate blue, that means he's got an eligible daughter."

"Yes sir, that could well be true," I answered.

That made this fellow as happy as a clam. He jumped back in his car, gave us all a wave and off he went. Ammon kept on painting until the car had passed over the second hill

up the way, clean out of sight. Then he turned around, threw
down his brush in disgust and shook his head.

"What did you lie to him for?" Ammon asked.

"I didn't," I responded. "I just didn't finish my sentence:
'Yes sir, that could well be true . . . but it's not.'"

Ammon has ten sons. One may be a bit peculiar, but
there's no girls ever come along at his house. Still, Ammon
was painting his gate blue for a very good reason that day.

In fact, Ammon was painting his gate blue for the same
reason Jake painted his blue. The same reason Levi painted
his blue and Noah painted his door blue. Blue paint was on
sale at K-Mart a month ago and all the boys stocked up.

Without the aid of lobbyists or public-relations people,
the Amish don't have any way to get the truth out to the public
as to what it really means to be Amish. We tend to let others
interpret our lives for the world to understand. Sometimes
even Hollywood takes a stab at the job. I believe the latest
intrusion into the Amish world from that neck of the woods
was a movie called *Witness*.

We don't go to the worldly amusements ourselves, things
like movie theaters, but we were by a neighbor's place a while
back. They're English, have a television and one of those VCR
things. Seeing as how they started the film after we got there,
we sort of figured it was just neighborly to watch a bit.

To be honest, I thought it a pretty good film about the
Pennsylvania Amish. They do a lot of things different than
around here, but it all was pretty good. I didn't see any need
for the violence and the adult situations, and after I'd watched
them three or four times, I'd say they were out of place, but it
wasn't a bad movie. What really surprised me was that it
wasn't what I thought of as a Hollywood movie.

If I was going to do something and put a Hollywood
label on it, I'd make it Hollywood. Instead of having an Amish

boy witness a murder in a big city, I'd have an Amishman commit the murder. He murders his wife, takes her out to the barn and then burns it down around her, claiming she had a heart attack.

To keep the same title, there is a witness. It would be this fellow's hired man, another Amishman who lives by the principle that you don't go around judging others so that you're not judged yourself. He'll never testify, living his life with a remembrance too horrible to speak of or to forget.

As the truth is revealed, our villain killed his wife because he's really a homosexual. He gets involved with drinking next, then drugs on the farm. He finally goes off to the Southwest and commits another murder before he's caught.

Now that is Hollywood, isn't it? The product of a vivid imagination. So vivid that you might find yourself with an Amish frame of mind some day, hoping that Eli, son of an Amish preacher, is never released from a Texas jail. Sometimes real life is much crazier than Hollywood.

We've heard that story for several years now, especially when we're up to Kidron for the Thursday livestock sale. For a while it seemed every week would find somebody adding a detail or two. Anymore I think it's just rumor, somebody says that somebody says and nobody knows what the facts have become.

Some say the craziness is over now, but I wonder. Eli is human, just like the rest of us. Being human, I wonder sometimes what evil does lurk in the mind. Even in the minds of some of the peaceful people, Our People, the Amish. How hard it is to live up to the rest of the world's notion of sainthood. Almost as hard as living up to our own.

Still, for all that could go wrong on a given day, this is the greatest country in the world, this United States. We've got no problem paying our taxes for the pleasure of being Americans. That's why, this being such a great country, it bothered us when we heard there were so many poor people in the United States today. It bothered us so much that Noah and I hitched up the buggy and went to town. We made a beeline right to the library and started to research. It didn't take long to discover some vital facts and determine exactly where that poverty line is. Hindsight says I'm sorry we did.

When we determined where the poverty level was, we also discovered we were beneath it. We're poor people, too. All this time under the notion we were quite happy, thank you. We've consoled ourselves with the knowledge that it's no sin to live in poverty these days. It is, however, a bit unhandy.

Maybe it was poverty that was the problem the last time I was to Berlin. Against my better judgment, I was in town doing some tourist watching. Right in the middle of uptown, right by the quilt shop, there was a big tour bus out of Pittsburgh, as I recall. Judging by what happened, it must have been loaded with poor people.

The bus door opened and a couple got off, man and woman. They go right over to the hitching post. She takes a stick and starts poking around. Next thing you know, he's got one of those Styrofoam coffee cups out of his pocket.

It is true as I am here, they proceed to load up that cup with horse droppings. He popped the lid on it and they trot right back on the bus. Can you imagine what it was like to ride back to the Keystone State with somebody too cheap to spend two dollars to buy fertilizer in a plastic bag? Tourists.

You know, though, our one experience with the tourist business down home has caused some to think. It was a few months ago, in the height of the heat, when tourism found us in a most unusual way.

Jake and Andy down at the mill had noticed the car making a circle or two of the building. When they heard the engine stop, they decided to take a peek out the back window. There, not twenty feet away, was a city woman rooting through the trash pile. In just a second or two, she pulls out a chicken crate and into the mill she comes. She walks right through the front door and says, "I want to buy this."

As I mentioned before, the language of the Amish home and society is what's called Pennsylvania Deutsch, a dialect of the German language. When we go to school, we learn English as a foreign language. Sometimes it's inconvenient, having to do all sorts of translating to do business with the English. Other times the Deutsch is a lifesaver.

Jake looks at Andy and in Deutsch says, "Buy? We're throwing that junk away."

Andy nodded, turned to the lady and in English said, "They're $10 each."

Poor Jake is choking on that one, especially when the woman wanted to dicker. Jake probably could have used a heart specialist when the price was finally set at $7.50.

Somewhere in the city of Columbus there is a woman who is very happy. Undoubtedly, in her living room she has decorated with a used, stinking chicken crate. As to Jake and Andy, the last time I was to the mill they were both going through the trash pile one more time seeing if there was anything else they might be able to sell.

Perhaps where all these tourist problems come from is the fact we've gotten spoiled. A family can go on vacation to Williamsburg or Disney World and see actors playing a part for their benefit. Folks who re-create a role, quit at five o'clock, get in their car and go back to normal living. Maybe the tourist ends up in Amish country expecting the same.

With forty thousand horse-and-buggy folk spread throughout Ohio and another sixteen thousand in Pennsylvania's Lancaster County alone, there's bound to be a few who are tourist-curious. I know an English who does a lot of business and traveling in Amish communities. He claims twenty-five percent of the Amish can't stand him, fifty percent can take or leave him and twenty-five percent are just as curious about him as he is about them.

It wasn't until long afterwards that I got the whole story, but this fellow was coming to see us one day. Being him, he makes a wrong turn. All of a sudden, the road he's on is going down into a valley. He knows this isn't right because we live on the ridge.

Fortunately, just ahead was an Amish farm, the man of the house out doing chores by the shed. The fellow in the car waved, the farmer waved back, so he stopped for directions.

"Say," the out-of-towner said, "I'm looking for E. R.'s place."

"E. R.'s place?" came the answer. The Amish have a habit of repeating a question not for being ignorant but to conserve breath in the long run. They want the answer right the first time they give it.

"If you're looking for E. R., you're on the wrong road."

The English put on his best rubber face and said, "I know that!"

This was about the funniest thing the Amish man had ever heard. It was so funny that both men had to mosey over to the nearby bench and take a rest. As they found their positions, the verbal jousting began.

"E. R.," the Deutscher went on, "he's quite a carpenter."

It became obvious the guest knew that already so that wasn't the purpose of the visit. The Amishman then started grabbing at straws, trying to figure out why this fellow wanted to see me.

"E. R.'s dad, he was a horse dealer, you know."

The English's stock soared to the moon when he acknowledged that he'd heard that, but he'd also heard it was my uncle who was the real horse trader. Several minutes passed as the Amishman proudly recalled some fine Belgians he'd owned.

"Say," the Amish asked, "you ever get over to the Dover draft colt sale?"

"No," the English said, shaking his head, "never been there. Been to the Topeka sale, though."

"That's it," the Amish cried out in excitement. "That's where I've seen you. I've seen you before. I knew it. Yep, the Indiana sale at Topeka, that's where it was. Last year, wasn't it?"

Instantly Tom, the English, knew his newfound friend was running a bluff. Tom had been to Topeka, sure enough, but it had been five years before. His Amish friend was apparently looking for common ground so this conversation could continue. Tom figured it best to play along, especially the way the Amish was enjoying the talk.

Five minutes, ten minutes and then fifteen minutes slid by. Both of them sitting there on the bench should have been poker players for all the bluffing each was doing. Tom was remembering all about a sale he wasn't at and the Amishman was filling in the details that he didn't know, either. The two of them proceeded to talk all the way around Robin Hood's barn and then back again. Tom was beginning to wonder if he was about to discover the Amishman had been sitting right next to him at the sale, the way the talk went. A lot of imagination used up to satisfy that human quirk known as curiosity.

Finally, after checking the license of the car and seeing it was from Columbus, the Amish asked, "From around here?"

Tom decided enough was enough. He clued this fellow in that he was coming to call because of our common interest in the genealogy. Before the Amishman could draw this one out, the door of the house opened and out came the lady of the farm.

Some say she didn't make any bones about it. She made a beeline to her husband and, in the Deutsch language, wanted to know who this fellow was and what he wanted. After sensing that Tom didn't understand the Deutsch, the farmer set his wife straight that Tom was all right.

Just like that, the lady switched to the English language and said, "I just come out to tell you the pies are out of the oven."

Of course it wouldn't be neighborly not to offer a slice of pie to a new friend. Once you got him in the house, then it's just polite to show off your own genealogy. Talk of this, talk of that and before you know it, four hours has slipped away.

I didn't say much to Tom when he finally got to the homeplace. Somehow I knew he'd had his ear talked off, having found one of those twenty-five percent of the Amish who is English-curious. I'd like to claim it's because I'm so perceptive about our neighbors, but there's another reason.

It took the Amishman, whose name is Mervin by the way and who also happens to be my cousin, four hours to give a set of directions that might have read, "Go to that crossroad fifty feet up there and turn right. If you go to the top of the hill, you might find that the guy who has been waving to us is named E. R." But who am I to deny a man his fun?

I hear a lot of folks say they'd like to see in an Amish house, they'd like to experience this or try that. In the Plain community, we've got no problem with that as long as folks remember one thing. We're not much on giving things away. We hold to the old, maybe outdated, notion you earn friendships.

Jonas was laid up in the Cleveland hospital for some time a few years back. I'm not sure what the problem was, the cure being quite lengthy. While he was up there, he just happened to make friends with Bill, an English guy in the next bed.

It may strike you as odd, but this friendship had nothing to do with the fact Bill and Jonas were different. It began when they discovered they had something in common. Come to find out, they both liked working with the wood for a hobby. Many the long hour was passed in that hospital room discussing the best way to turn a maple bar on the lathe.

One thing led to another after they both were released and Jonas extended the welcome for Bill to come our way. Bill, he never married, so maybe it was all the better he took to Jonas and the family. A visit now and then turned into pretty regular company. It was like both sides benefited each visit. Bill would learn about the Plain People and Jonas was finding out them city people don't bite.

It came Christmastime last year and Bill had made his way to what he was now calling his adopted home at Jonas's. The celebration of our Lord's birth is a festive occasion in our homes, but without those silly decorations. No time for the tree or lights, but we don't mind a fine gift or two to go with the party.

Gifts were exactly what Bill came toting that day. Oh, you should have seen the excitement when the boys discovered those baseball bats and gloves were for them. The girls cleaned up as well with so many art and sewing supplies. Jonas got himself a great genealogy book and one on woodworking, too, and Ruth, the lady of the house, was well pleased with the bolt of material and the tub of fancy popcorn just for her.

Bill was feeling awfully good with all that excitement. Some claim it was the best family feeling he'd ever had. It was so good an emotion that he never noticed Ruth slip out of the living room and return with a package of her own.

The Amish have to justify the usefulness of a gift before they give it. It was with more than a little tenderness that Ruth said, "We got you this, just in case you ever decide to come where you belong."

As the paper fell away, Bill couldn't believe it. Jonas had been to the buggymakers and bought a lap blanket, in a red tartan, just like theirs. That's family for sure and I don't think Bill will have much problem remembering that.

Making Amish friends does have a high price, though. If you'd be making friends with the buggy crowd, then you have to put up with some of the world's greatest schemers. Some claim the Amish are so quiet because they're up to something all the time. One thing for sure, you'd just better be on your toes when you come down to the Peoli Valley.

Dick is a fellow from Zanesville that's a lot like Bill. He's an English who just sort of took to the Amish. He's been pretty good to all of us, but that doesn't mean he's exempt from us taking advantage of him.

It was the morning of the big horse sale down at the

County Fairgrounds when Dick came driving down the Peoli
Road. He pulled into Noah's lane just as Noah was coming out
the back door, putting on his hat and coat.

"Dick, good to see you. I was just going to hitch up and
go down to the grocery. Since you're here . . ."

See what I mean by the scheming? Dick's used to it so he
motioned Noah into the truck. Off they went, Noah chitter-
chatting away like some kid.

They'd just about finished grocery shopping when
around the corner in the store came Lester. That's Noah's little
brother, the one still living at home with the old folks.

"Dick, we knew you'd be coming our way," went Lester.
"Dad's here and we was thinking. Maybe you could stop by
the home place and give us a lift to the sale?"

More scheming, to be sure. As dearly as Dick loves them
all, though, he's not going to be the county taxi for the Amish.
He begged off, got Noah out of there and headed back to the
house.

When they got home, Noah jumped out and rushed those
groceries inside real quick. He's back before Dick has turned
the truck around and gasps, "Miriam wants you to be here for
noon dinner, you know."

"Well, I suppose," Dick goes, sort of teasing Noah, "but I
might be late. That is, unless you go to that sale with me."

Noah looks at Dick a second, turns around and runs, not
walks but runs, back in the house. In just a second, here he
comes out the door with the three boys. In about four strides,
Noah was around the truck and they were all inside, everybody ready to go.

It was a good sale, hundreds of head changing hands and
several thousand folks to visit with. It might have been even a
great sale for Dick except for Noah. Every fifteen minutes, as
regular as a clock himself, Noah would ask Dick what time it
was.

It was odd at first, then funny and had finally reached the annoying stage at eleven-forty-five. That's when Noah figured it was time to head home, but he cautioned Dick not to rush it. It was easier to talk in a slower-moving vehicle, he said.

Talk Noah did, all the way home. Dick thought his ear was about to fall off. It wouldn't have been so bad, but Noah just seemed to be rambling. Dick did think it peculiar, but Noah had done peculiar things before.

The Amish aren't anything for that Social Security, taking care of their own elderly. Right next to Noah's place lives his grandmother. As they turned into the lane, Dick couldn't help notice a couple of buggies at Grandma's hitching post.

"Look there," said Noah shaking his head. "Grandma must have more company again. She'll be ninety-three next year. I sure hope we get company like that when we're old farts like her."

Something about an Amishman calling his grandmother an old fart hit Dick as being so out of character it was funny. Dick started laughing and laughing and just about got hysterical. Noah just shrugged it off, jumped out of the truck with the boys, trotted up the steps and disappeared into the house.

When Dick composed himself, he crawled out of the truck, still wiping tears out of his eyes. He was grinning as he climbed the steps and opened the door. Opened the door and was hit by the most wondrous smell of dinner.

It was magnificent, the aroma of homemade everything. There was chicken, potatoes, beans, bread, everything. It was such a great smell that Dick didn't notice at first something was wrong. There wasn't any noise in the house, and Noah has six children.

Very carefully, Dick tiptoed through the mudroom, past the kitchen and peeked around the corner into the living room. There, across the way, stood Noah, Miriam and the six children all lined up like steps. Along with them stood Noah's dad, the one from the store, his mother, brothers, sisters, wives, husbands and children. One of those CPA types would of counted seventy-eight Amish. All together at one time, in one place, because they had to tell Dick some things.

Things like Miriam seeing Dick coming up the road that morning and telling Noah whatever it took, keep him out of the house. Or that brother Lester didn't want to go to the auction, nor did his dad. For that matter, neither did Noah. Or the fact the buggies at the post weren't there visiting Grandma, they were the ones the family didn't have space to hide in the barn.

Maybe it wasn't something Noah's family had to tell Dick, now that I think on it. Maybe it was more something Dick had to be reminded of. That they did the only way they could, singing one of the best renditions of "Happy Birthday" ever heard. Poor Dick, he'd waited thirty-seven years for a surprise party and then it was the Amish who threw it. Schemers, connivers and the greatest people on earth.

10

A little bit of humanity

It wasn't but maybe six or seven months later that Dick walked a fine line flirting with disaster. He was to Noah's one spring day, just as two brand-new self-propelled lawn mowers were being unloaded from the boxes. Spring housecleaning of the yard was about to begin.

Noah's two oldest boys could hardly wait to see how these beauties would run. Chores may be work to some but, believe it or not, there are some who do enjoy a good day's effort. Dick watched the excitement mount before he tossed in a novel thought.

"You know," he said, "when I had a self-propelled mower, I had this idea one day. I put a stake in the center of the yard and then tied a rope between the stake and the mower. I just fired it right up, pulled up a chair and sat there, smoking my pipe and watching the mower going around cutting the whole yard."

They all got a little chuckle out of that before Noah motioned the boys off to work. He waited until they had gotten completely out of earshot before he said, "You know they're going to try that."

Dick nodded and said, "Why do you think I mentioned it?"

Probably a month had gone by before Dick was back in town on a little business. From a block away, he spied Noah coming for him, waving with both arms to get Dick's attention. As fast as a man can walk, Noah beaded right in on Dick.

"Dick, don't come by the house for a while."

"Why's that Noah? We're the best of friends."

"True, but the rope broke."

This didn't make a whole lot of sense to Dick until Noah refreshed his memory.

"The boys tried your trick for cutting the grass. Putting a stake out and letting the mower run itself. It worked pretty good the first time. Second time as well. Then, during the third try, the rope let go.

"It wouldn't have been so bad but it let go right as the mower was pointed to Grandma's flower bed. Or what used to be the flower bed.

"She's looking for you, so maybe you should just lay low."

Dick took that advice and steered clear a good three months. He figured that was plenty of time for things to cool down and memories to fade. He was right for the most part. Grandma mashed him only once with her cane.

Flower gardens like hers are a virtual essential to the good Amish homestead. That's Momma's hobby and she'll make it a real burst of color. For the most part, that just might be the only hobby she does take to. It's pretty obvious by now that I haven't discussed much of the role of our womenfolk. There's a good reason for that—I don't know what all they're into. One thing for sure, it keeps them busy.

All in all, down our road you're going to find a pretty good bunch of mothers, housekeepers and seamstresses. I sure would like to be able to tell you what makes Nettie such a good cook or why Ruth can stitch so nice, but I always get run off before I can find out. It's really true that the kitchen and the sewing room are in Mom's kingdom and the menfolk don't need to get underfoot.

What's not true is that such things as quilting bees, those social gatherings among the ladies of the area, are strictly for fun. I heard some tourists talking once in Winesburg about those poor Amish women. They were saying, proving how dumb they were more than anything else, that the women's only amusement was gabbing at a quilting. Granted there's a great deal of socializing going on, but that quilt is being put in to be used. We all remember how cold it got a few years back, those quilts feeling real good right then. Come to think of it, that was the cold before the baby boom around here.

That thinking on hobbies carries over to the men as well. There's any number around who like to work with the wood. It's not that they want to hang the shingle out for the tourist, but you never can tell when another piece of furniture might be necessary. Mervin was three legs done on a highchair before he realized why his wife had asked him to make it.

I'm not saying furniture needs are all that great around home anyway. Dad will have an overstuffed chair for himself and Mom will have a smaller version. Maybe a nice couch and some straight-back chairs will fill out the rest of the seating needs. Of course there's a dining room table, and chairs there, too, but perhaps it's more noticeable what the Amish do without.

You'll not find the carpet man getting much business with the Plain People. A throw runner, rag or hooked, does real nice. Not much for the decorations, either, other than a calendar or two and maybe a few religious sayings carved on a plaque. Pretty simple, going along with a simple life.

Even the heat and lights tend to run to the simple back home. Remember, we don't go for the electricity. Our hillbilly neighbors heat with the wood and read by the candle or oil lantern. We let the propane take care of all that for us, whether it be for the lights or appliances. If only they could invent the propane microwave oven . . .

Yep, it's a simple life. It probably would be a lot simpler if there wasn't the rest of the world. You try to walk the straight and narrow, but then things of the world jump right out in front of you. Take what happened to Jake's cousin Levi.

Levi don't live around here, living a lot farther north, up east of Cleveland. He's in that Old Order crowd up towards Burton. He farms and is a faithful sort, but he's also sort of curious about the city of Cleveland itself.

A while back, Levi talked his neighbor, an English, into giving him a ride into town. It seems this English works there someplace. Levi had a little time on his hands and decided he needed a little vacation. Off they went one morning, one to work and the other just to look around.

Five o'clock comes and Levi meets his friend at the appointed place. He had a good day, didn't see all that much that was so great, but he did appreciate the lift. They made their way home and the English didn't think any more about it. At least not until the evening news came out.

The lead story that night on the local news at six was that the police had raided one of those houses of ill repute. They had film on the cops leading people out of this building. Then they panned over the crowd of spectators.

It was a rough-looking crowd, but it was the roughest side of town. A real sin city. Maybe to some there wasn't any as rough looking as the guy standing right in the middle of the front row of the spectators. The one with the long black hair, the beard but no mustache and the black felt hat. The one named Levi.

Every once in a while you might see Amish people riding around in a van. If you're buggy-bound and have to go great distances, that's the preferred means of travel. Hiring a van and driver is not cheap, running at least fifty cents a mile and sometimes more, so you'll always see those vans full. Fifty cents a mile split twenty ways is a lot easier on the pocketbook.

The pocketbook was what I was thinking of when a letter came from far northwest of here about a job for my carpenters. It sounded pretty good, good enough to take a look, but fifty cents a mile was going to be costing me too much. After a little thought, I decided to do something wild and hitchhike.

When I told Abe, my second in command on the crew, what I was up to, you should have heard him hoot.

"You can't be doing that," he was saying. "There's a lot of crazy people out driving around."

"I know that," I said, "but there's a lot of crazy people hitchhiking, too."

You could see it in Abe's eyes that he thought of me in that light. He nodded, accepting the truth in my words, and said, "Have a good trip."

The next morning I got a car-driving neighbor to give me a lift over to the interstate. I was trying to lay low as Our People aren't much for hitching rides. Nothing's ever been said, but it is accepting charity and we're not much for that. It's also getting close to the English world as well. I was still weighing these negatives as I hopped out of Brian's car, got in position and held up my thumb.

Those who speak of that luck of the Irish are off by only two letters. With the luck of the Amish, within one minute's time I was in the cab of one of those big semi trucks. Not only

was he heading in my direction, he was going right past
where I wanted to be. Quite an enjoyable ride, I might note,
talking of this and that.

The luck held at the project site as well. It was an easy job
and I put in a bid I thought to be pretty high. Within an hour
I was walking back to the roadway with not only the contract
in my pocket, but a promise of some more business headed
our way.

I was thinking I should have been a big-time gambler,
with all my luck, when the second truck I saw stopped to give
me a ride toward home. I was well pleased when the driver
said his last stop was about two miles from the home place. If
I'd be willing to wait while he made a few stops, I'd be eating
supper right on time.

The stops he had to make didn't bother me, but might
bother some. I was riding in the carcass truck, going to different livestock farms and picking up the dead cattle. Bob's final
destination was the rendering plant in our neck of the woods.
At least the ride was convenient.

It was the first stop we made, down south of where I'd
been, that things got real interesting. We just pulled into the
livestock barn when an Amishman came walking around the
corner. As I've mentioned, whenever two or more Amish join
together, good talk breaks out. I hopped out of that truck and,
even though I'd never seen this fellow before, talk we did.

Bert, that was his name, seemed to be pretty friendly as
we loaded a hide into the truck. We talked a little bit before he
looked at me and said, "Where you coming from?"

I told him I'd been to Medina County and he said, "I
thought so. Medina County? I know your brother."

"You do?" I asked.

"Oh yes," goes Bert, "he came over from Lodi not long
ago. One of them Swartzentruber Amish there. I bought some

heifers from him. Good price. You see him, send him back. We can do some more business."

I nodded that I would and then said, "How do you know that was my brother? You don't even know my name, other than E. R."

"Don't kid me," Bert goes, "you guys are almost twins. You look alike, talk alike, walk alike and there's not too many of us with blue eyes."

I couldn't argue with that. At any rate, the fellow with the truck was ready to go, so I said my good-byes. We'd gone maybe a mile or two on down the road when Bob, the driver, asked, "What does your brother do?"

"I don't know," I answered honestly.

"Oh," he said, "I understand. I guess Amish families don't always stay that close."

"No, that's not it. I don't have a brother."

This fellow just about wrecks the truck in surprise and then blurted out, "Why did you tell Bert you did?"

"I didn't tell Bert," I answered. "He told me."

If it's not the thrill of finding a long-lost relative you never had, then sometimes it's all the excitement this statewide lottery Ohio has that can get a community all fired up. It wasn't too many weeks back that the pot grew to more millions than a man can count. I'm not for that, nor are others, for it's gambling but, should somebody else win and share the benefit, that's worth thinking about.

Thinking about it we were, down at the mill one rainy Thursday when driver Joe was ready to divide up money he never won. He wanted to know, though, should he really win, what we'd all want.

Freeman thought about it and then said, "I always wanted to be a farmer, but I'm not greedy. You can get me the farm this year. Next year, with the next check, you can get me the cows."

We got a laugh out of that and then Joe turned to Ivan, Freeman's brother, and asked him what he'd want.

Without a second's thought, Ivan says, "A Cadillac."

Such a statement was like dropping a bomb on all of us, for Ivan is a pillar of the church. All his life Ivan had been buggy-bound. Here he is, shaking us all up saying such a thing and he wasn't done.

"Not any Cadillac," he went on, "a great big one. One I can drive around in. One I can put those big whitewalls on and the fuzzy stuff on the dash. Since I've got a November birthday, I'll put a big Scorpio decal on the rear window. Last, but not least, I'll trade my black felt church hat for one of those purple ones with a white feather in it.

"Just think, the first Amish pimp."

Seems somebody else has been to the big city more than he admits to, but I'm not naming names.

It was just a few months ago when I heard some distressing news about the affairs of the world. It seems there was a United States congressman from Ohio who was relieved of his elected position. According to the story we got, this fellow got into an elevator there in the Congress building and couldn't keep his hands off the young lady who was running the thing.

I reflected on this and found it disturbs me a great deal. I feel bad a man would have such a weakness and hope he receives treatment as soon as possible. I feel worse for the young lady, one who should be entitled to her privacy. What I find most aggravating, though, is the whole situation our country finds itself in.

I suppose I should be glad we're not for the running-for-public-office notion. Can you imagine all these representatives, from all over the United States, looking out for our best interests and they're too dumb to run an elevator by themselves? They got to hire somebody to do it for them. I had that figured out about the first time I was ever in the thing, but I'm not saying anything about it. We've got a senator coming up for reelection and I'd hate for folks to think I might be as smart as he is.

Once in a while, not often but on occasion, maybe the Amish do initiate a few problems of their own. Everybody is trying to lead a solid life, but humanity does creep in. It's not that we go looking for trouble, but it does find some of us.

There was a fellow who went up from the Peoli Valley to Sugarcreek once. He shopped around a bit before he came across a clothing store. Tucked way in the back, this place had a whole selection of Amish straw hats. By that I mean most of those thirteen styles of local Amish people I mentioned earlier were represented.

This was an absolute bonanza for this fellow because collecting hats was his hobby. True, even though he was loyal to one faction, he had collected the hat worn by just about every faction. The one his collection was missing was the rounded crown and wider brim of the Andy Weaver bunch. Sure enough, in front row center, there one was.

The hat was purchased in the blink and off this fellow goes. Since it just happened to be a bright, sunny day, he figured he'd give this new hat a test drive. He put his old hat in the bag, put the new one on and strolled up to the corner.

Just as he reached that corner, a buggy pulled up to the traffic light. Naturally, with this fellow's luck, the young ladies on board were of the local Andy Weaver congregation. They looked over, recognized him not to be one of their own and proceeded to toss their heads in righteous indignation.

When this didn't have the desired effect of making the fellow slink away in guilt, the young lady holding the lines took the next step of disapproval. She stuck her tongue out at me.

It could be I've been around too many English or maybe I just wasn't thinking at the moment. Considering the scene, I did what came natural. I gave her the finger.

Before I could realize what I'd done, made this horribly obscene gesture at these two pious, devout Christian girls, they both gave it back with both hands. They pulled away in a huff, sure this impostor was insane. As for me, all I could do was stand and shake my head. Not at the impropriety, nor at our transgression. No, I could only shake my head at how worldly we people apart can be sometimes.

Maybe it's not as bad, and maybe it's worse, the mess I got into earlier this year. A friend, an English, is a big shot with the American Red Cross over northwest of here. As I think on it, it was June when he came driving up our lane.

I told Henry it was a little early for the blood drive, but that wasn't it. It seemed his chapter of the Red Cross had a project. A poor family in his area had had a fire and nothing but bad luck since. The Red Cross set their caps to it and found a church to fund the supplies. Then one of the wise ones went to his neighbors and rounded up a work crew. It was because of this work crew that I fit into the equation.

They were the Amish of Henry's area, a little more liberal than around here, and all were farmers. Not a carpenter among them. What Henry had come looking for was a boss, estimating the project and seeing it through to the end. It must have taken me three minutes to get my tools, a few clothes and off we went.

I don't get to Henry's much, it being way too far by the buggy. Maybe the car is more convenient, covering the same space in two hours what would take me three days, but we don't need such a thing for our own use. It was good to visit at his place, though, before we headed out to the project.

It must have taken me twenty minutes to get this one figured out. That sort of worried me, the job looking so simple. I put the tape on everything again. They called in my list to the lumberyard and we headed off to Henry's to wait for the morning and get this one done.

We got on the job about eight that next morning. The lumberyard had already delivered the materials and it wasn't but fifteen minutes before a van came down the street carrying the work crew. They piled out, chatted a bit, had me divvy up the job and the work began.

These boys might be farmers for a living but they did a good impression of carpenters this day. They worked hard and they worked the way I wanted it to be. I wasn't having a single problem until about ten that morning.

That's when one of the farmers came over and mentioned we were running a little short on two-by-fours. About forty short, in fact. That might not have bothered me, anybody making a mistake and such, but an hour later we were four hundred feet short of pine board.

I was sure smelling fish without an ocean nearby. It was against my better nature, but I went ahead and called the lumberyard again. They sort of kidded me a bit, me calling first for more two-by-fours and now for pine stock. They asked if I wanted to stay on the line in case something else came up, but I was thinking I'd better get back to the job. A feeling that the cat was about to get out of the bag was gnawing at me.

Sure enough, just before dinner, one of the younger fellows I'd been friendly with stopped to visit a bit. After some of this and that, he said, "Say, when the project is over, you take all the excess home with you for your crew, don't you?"

I just shook my head, knowing what was coming next.

"Oh," he went on, "then maybe we could make you a good price on what's left over?"

There was a meeting held right after dinner that day. There weren't any raised voices or threats, nothing like that. Only firm words. I don't know who planned on building what that day, but it never happened. By the time the day ended, the project done and those farmers' eyes on their shoes whenever I looked at them, it just happened we managed to have forty two-by-fours and four hundred feet of pine stock left over. Really can't begrudge a good try, though.

Far be it from me to be all too critical of those fellows, considering what happened up in Holmes County two months back. I didn't start the trouble but, well, maybe I'd just better explain.

I'd gone visiting to cousin Jake's for the weekend. When some unexpected company arrived to spend the day, we decided we'd slip on down to one of those cheese factories and pick up some nibbling food. Jake and I hitched up the buggy and headed off, giving me a chance to find out more about his unusual visitors.

The guests were some of Ohio's New Order Amish, a bunch that separated from the Old Order around 1967–69. I'd seen their kind of buggies before, the ones with sliding doors and rubber-rimmed wheels, but I'd never had a chance to see some up close. Different, to say the least, but I'm not saying there's all that wrong with that, either.

The women seem to like the brighter colors, still plain-pattern dresses, but lighter hues than we see around Peoli. The girls aren't above having an opinion of their own, either, I might note. Could be, should more of Holmes County take to this concept, there might be a little less of the old-man's-word-is-the-law thinking before long.

The fellows were different, too, especially having English haircuts. For me to get a trim, all that's required is a bowl and the shears. These fellows had the hair cut around the ears, nice and neat. The beards were shorter, too, and in fact, one fellow said he wasn't growing one until he married. Unusual for Ohio, where we've always wore the whiskers as soon as they'd grow after baptism.

What I found really unusual was that the New Orders have church every other Sunday like we do, but then have Sunday School on the off-Sundays. The young people have Wednesday night fellowship as well, a novel idea to me. As fine as this family seemed to be, there must be something to this sort of thinking.

I complimented Jake on his choice of friends and commented how little I knew about this New Order. We got to talking about all those factions of the Amish, feeling sorry some sociologist, anthropologist or some other ologist of some sort don't put out a book on the subject. We figured should the author split enough hairs like those who are book-learning smart tend to do, this text should be about the size of an encyclopedia.

Jake was saying he'd read the Amish population was growing about six percent each year. Even with migration and losing some to the world, Our People expect to be near one hundred thousand strong in this state alone within my lifetime. If we throw in the way the Amish are spreading all across the country, we just might see half a million horse-and-buggy types across the Americas before we're done. Maybe someday all folks would have daily contact with the Amish and we wouldn't be such a tourist novelty. Such an encyclopedia just might have some value, but it will take a smart one to write it. That sure lets out everybody I know.

At any rate, we got down there to the cheese place and you should have seen the tourists. Fourteen busloads we counted and the cars, too, all there to buy cow by-products, as Jake calls it. We got in line with the rest of them, made our selection and shuffled over to the counter.

Just as I put the cheese on the scale, the girl running the place asks, "Do you ship your milk here?"

I was going to say no, being a carpenter and not a local farmer, when I felt Jake's size-twelve boot pressing on the top of my size sevens. More out of pain than anything else, I grimaced.

She must of mistook my squint for a yes, for she said, "All right, what's your name?"

I looked at Jake, but he was busy inspecting the ceiling tile at the moment. It was pretty obvious I was going to sink or swim on my own. I figured I'd better play this one pretty safe, using the Amish equivalent of John Smith.

"It's Mose Yoder, " I go.

Jake did keep a straight face while the girl got out her lists. She runs down through and then looks up all confused.

"There's sixteen Mose Yoders on this list. Which one are you?"

Jake leans over, acting like he's checking the list, and goes, "I think he's the second one there."

The next thing you know, I'm signing "Mose Yoder" on a blank and getting a discount on our cheese. I knew right then it's forgery, theft, fraud and just about every other crime known to man, all for twenty-five percent off. I know it and I felt bad about it. Bad enough to say something, but only outside.

I tapped Jake and said, "What did you make me do that for?"

Jake shook his head. "I'm not the one telling my name is Mose Yoder."

I wouldn't of felt so bad if, since I was taking all the guilt, I'd get all the cheese. It didn't come out that way, Jake eating his share plus some. He ate so much he wanted me to go back with him and get some more.

Can you believe it? Larceny and then he wants me to be a part of it again. I can just tell you one thing. It worked the second time, too.

11

And a whole lot more

It's really not far off to say that Mose Yoder down home is just like John Smith in Cleveland or Columbus. The Amish have a very limited number of last names, Yoder probably being most common. Then Miller, Weaver, Troyer, Stutzman, Schlabach, Hershberger and a few others, including Beachy.

First names aren't too much more numerous. The Amish are partial to the Biblical names and Moses leads the pack again. Down home, just like in most Amish communities, it's not at all unusual to find six Mose Yoders, all on the same road.

The worldly types probably aren't seeing any problem yet, figuring everybody then goes by their middle name. Well, that is precisely the problem, for with the exception of the New Order crowd, the Amish don't have middle names.

Dad's Roy so my middle initial is R. He's Amos's boy, so Dad is Roy A. If I would of been blessed with children, their middle names would be E. The middle name is actually an initial, the first letter of your father's first name becoming your

120

middle name, boys and girls alike. Not to worry, though, about any confusion over having six Mose A. Yoders along the same road. The Amish figured it out years ago and that's precisely why they invented nicknames.

Sure enough, Hardware Mose works in the store selling nails and Potato Mose grows the spuds down on the farm. It's a custom that carries over everywhere, whether your name is common or not. All it takes is for you to get your foot, or your fork, caught in your mouth one time.

As good as supper was that night at Junior's, I'd never tasted a dessert like those sponge cakes with the cream fillings that were served. One was good, the second one better and I was still in the mood for more six later. It wasn't until I'd polished off the whole box before Junior threw down his fork in disgust. "That's the dumbest thing I ever saw," he said, looking right at me.

"What?" I answered, being the clever one I am.

"You've been eating the best of Amish cooking," he said, shaking his head. "Fresh everything, food that tourist people would pay a fortune to sample. Chickens died for you today. All that and you proceed to eat a whole box, my only box, of dessert. I never seen the like of it."

If you come our direction asking for E. R., you'll be headed off in four directions. Ask for the Beachy place and there's five possibilities. Ask for Twinkie and they'll tell you exactly where I can be found.

I've always enjoyed eating parties like that one myself. In fact, I would of had a grand time last June when we got together to remind Jake of another year passing except for one detail. My cousin Maryann brought that growth she's married to.

Calling him a growth is the only label fit. Grandma Stutzman, who died at ninety-seven, I might note, enjoyed every day of her poor health. This guy doesn't enjoy it, he relishes every second of misery and then insists on sharing all this grief with the rest of us.

Abe has been sick every time I've seen him since he married Maryann and that's been twenty years now. One year it was terminal gout, the next year the grippe set in. This year it was the shingles. It was bad enough to hear about it, but then the dumb one had to pull up his shirt to show us. Right there at the dinner table he does this. It was the first time I'd gagged on food since the rhubarb incident.

Some often wonder if there's certain foods the Amish don't take to, like those friends of ours of the Jewish persuasion. For the most part, every Deutschman I know is on that seafood diet plan: see food and eat it. Of course, being human beings, there are exceptions to the rule. Jake don't like green beans and Ammon says if his wife fixes potato casserole once more he'll scream. As for me, it's the rhubarb.

Oh, Sis was growing up those many years ago. She was trying hard to be mother's helper, fixing the meals and graduating on to making pies that one June. That evening after Dad and I had come home from work, she sure did set out a spread.

Sis could cook and it sure filled me up. Even at that, there's always room for dessert around an Amish home. Dad sliced up a big piece of pie for himself while I took my share as well. It sure looked good, so I launched in with a heaping forkful.

About the time that pie hit my taste buds, I felt my mouth puckering inside out. My eyes started watering and then rolling around in my head. I thought I might be at the end of my days, especially looking over at Dad, peacefully chewing away on his piece.

Those United Nations diplomats could have taken lessons from Dad on glossing over disasters. He got that first piece chewed up and swallowed. There wasn't a tear, a gag or any other sign of pain as he said, "Leah, pie just the way it ought to be made. You didn't add sugar so I can put in just what I want."

Isn't it strange, though, that if he was so crazy about the pie, he sure was standoffish about having the rest of mine. As a matter of fact, as I recall it now, he always checked to see who made dessert after that. As for me, if I was ever in the wilderness, surrounded by nothing but rhubarb stalks, all I can say is I'd better get rescued soon.

I hope Ohio's prison system don't cater to the rhubarb themselves for I just might be headed there myself if my next adventure don't turn out so well. Could be that I'll be using the alias Twinkie or maybe even Mose Yoder at the time. At any rate, Levi and I are thinking about stealing a barn. Not the whole barn, mind you, just the back wall. What we're going to do with it after that is beyond us right now, but something. After all, to some of us around here, this back wall of that barn is just about sacred.

It's just a few miles northwest of us, this treasure, standing on a Swartzentruber farm. It's just another barn to the old fellow who lives there. For the life of him, he can't figure out what is so interesting about a wall that's got a nice big bull's-eye carved on it.

According to the story, the family who owned the place before the Amish were good folks. Good, except one son was nothing for farm work. It doesn't cut any ice with the Swartzentrubers that the young fellow would rather throw rocks at this target he'd carved than plow or do his choring.

It doesn't matter to them that the boy, Denton by name, got good enough throwing the rocks to try throwing baseballs over in Newcomerstown. Once he started doing that, he wasn't anything at all for the farm work. As a matter of fact, it wasn't too long before Denton left the area altogether.

This Swartzentruber's parents bought the place a few years later. The Amishman, an old man now, has lived his entire life on that ground never knowing what happened to worthless Denton.

Levi and I know, though. Seems we've read enough and heard enough to know Denton did play ball for Newcomerstown. He did good, good enough to take a chance. Denton borrowed some money, bought a suit of clothes and took a trip up to Cleveland.

All those rocks thrown at that barn wall must have had some value after all. It seems once Denton got a chance, major league baseball never saw a ball thrown so fast. As fast as a cyclone in fact.

Denton the cyclone. Denton Cyclone Young. Cy Young, the winningest pitcher in baseball history and it all started a few miles from right here. I've never seen one of those big-time ball games, but oh, I'd like to have that target. Just something about a memory, however you care to imagine it, that's wonderful.

We've already had the law looking for some Amish in these parts, so maybe Levi and I wouldn't be so unique. Oh my, yes, we've got ourselves a desperate criminal type right here in our community, at least according to some. That rascal Leroy, the one with the sawmill, is our equivalent of a Dillinger, being so ruthless that he burns scraps of oak lumber in his yard.

That's right, burning that sweet-smelling excess from his wood shop in an orderly pile is such a crime that our environmental protection people threatened Leroy with a $25,000 fine and a year in jail if he didn't stop, and stop right now. It didn't matter folks have been burning wood along this road for almost two hundred years. It didn't matter that the rendering plant, the one right by Valley Ridge School, puts out plenty of stink and now wants to burn rubber tires, too. No sir, it was

Leroy who was the criminal and he simply had to be stopped.

To say this caused some worry with Leroy, as well as the rest of us, is one of the year's biggest understatements. Being simple people, we know our words can't be heard for all the shouting of lawyers or government types. Even though it seemed like these enforcement people were just looking for an easy case to help their statistics, which don't seem too fair, there wasn't appearing to be too much we could do about this mess.

Just about the time we were all feeling pretty low about this, a stranger came calling in our neck of the woods. Mike was his name, a young fellow who asked some questions and then listened even more. We thought he might be from the government at first and were sort of standoffish. When we found out he was a newspaper reporter, that was a little better but still a lot of lips remained buttoned shut. We're a private people for the most part and more than one wondered what this Mike was up to.

He visited there at Leroy's and got some of the facts. Some say they saw him later looking at that stink plant. Others saw him watching Amos turning the soil with that magnificent team of Belgians he has. One or two even say Mike was seen watching school let out, seeing children who are miniature versions of their parents head for home right past what we call pollution but the government calls business.

It was maybe two weeks later when Leroy's got a copy of some big-city newspaper in the mail. They thought it strange, not subscribing to such or even having heard of it before. As a matter of fact, I heard they almost threw it away when Junior spotted something about an Amishman and the government.

Sure enough, Mike the reporter had gotten the story into print. I saw the paper and I'd hold to the opinion those bureaucrats didn't end up looking too good. More like fools, come to think of it. Maybe that's why it wasn't but a day or two before they made a real quick peace with Leroy and haven't been seen around these parts since.

As to Mike, we haven't seen him around here, either. I'll tell you I'd say he's more than welcome, but maybe it's just he's a bit shy. Like so many others, he could be thinking the Amish world is bound to family, and outsiders need not apply. I'll tell you, like I'd tell him, sometimes things around here are a matter of the heart more than blood. We'll keep a slice of pie handy in case Mike Hardin ever realizes that.

Funny, but some of the best stories within an Amish community come from those outside it. Maybe it's the old forest for the trees thing that clouds the vision around here sometimes. Mike comes from a city newspaper and closes a big can of worms. Even that thing about Cy Young and his barn, we wouldn't of known about it except we happened to have been talking to our local highway patrolman a while back. Walter had seen us playing ball over at the school and thought we'd like to hear that wonderful tale. It was a good one, but then again so was Walt.

Walt was a big ox in that gray uniform. He just looked like he wouldn't take no lip from nobody. I think the whole county was afraid of him for about a week. Then we found out the biggest thing about him was his heart.

More than one night Walt would follow an Amish teenager, a little deep in the jug, all the way home. He'd keep his lights flashing the whole way, taking care of what he called "my boys." It was no happy day when Walt was transferred on to another post.

It was even a sadder day last January when news came through the mail that Walt had passed away. He'd suffered with cancer, even when he was here, never sharing a moment's pain. There was no better man, unless it's my dad, who ever lived around here, and the whole thing needed to be thought out.

I spent most of an hour up on top of the hill behind the house. It's my place to be alone, to think on things and air some things out. The hilltop is my private place to regret all the things I never said until it was too late. It was drizzling a bit but I never felt it as I looked to the north, out over Troyer's farm.

I take a great stock in the fact that in our Father's house there are many mansions. I don't want to be putting words in our Lord's mouth or stepping out of line, but standing up there surveying the valley sure can make you hope. Looking over Troyer's made me hope all the more.

The way I'm wishing, when that day comes, where one life ends and another begins, I'll be lucky enough to find myself heading up a long gravel lane. If you'd bear to the right, up the hill, you'd head to the house. The women will be there, Grandma and the rest, doing this and that. I'll be there before long to do some visiting, but there's some business first.

The lane bends left to the barn, right through the playground. I'll linger a second or two; Mary's Miriam is there, her suffering over now. I'll want to smile at the twins, the ones who never had a chance to feel the love that Mom and I saved just for them. I'll linger, but only for a moment.

It's to the far side of the barn I'm headed. Over to the shady side, under the overhang. That's where you'll find the long, low bench. Grandpa is already there, along with Unk, Daniel's dad, too, and Walt just taking a seat. I can almost hear them saying, "Good to see you boy. Sit down, rest for eternity and tell us the one about . . ."

The sound of my name being called brought me back to reality. I turned around and looked to the house. The girl I married one April 2 was waving me down the hill for supper.

With my idea of the afterlife gone for the moment and a smile on my face, I headed down to the woman of my dreams.

How exciting it is to wait for tomorrow in the paradise we live in today. How thrilling today to dream of the paradise our Lord has made for us, knowing how beautiful it will be. Sort of hard to be sad with that to carry along in your heart every single day.

If there's been one thing I've wanted to get across in our visit, it's the Amish are people. Of all the other things so many talk about, weddings, funerals, why we're not so keen on the photos or whatever, the only point is that Amish country is made up of people, not animals in a zoo or circus freaks. Sometimes we forget but, being real people, there's real vice even in the Plain People.

Tobacco has a market among the Plain People, smoking and chewing the leaf alike. Around the home place the rule was that if I'd refrain from chewing until my eighteenth birthday, Grandpa's gold pocket clock would be mine. I'm pleased to report that I achieved that objective, that timepiece ticking in my pocket. As a matter of fact, the chew never was for me even as an adult. I might note, though, before some think wrong, that nobody ever said anything about learning to smoke a pipe.

As many smokers that there are in those buggies, there must be twice as many who indulge in another vice. Grandma Beachy at the age of ninety-four did not need glasses. No sir, she drank it right out of the bottle. It's a sad fact that some Amish imbibe a bit too much. Some end up in Alcoholic Anonymous, others like Ivan. He's the best barn builder in Ohio, but he doesn't work much these days. I'm not one to say it's a sickness, but it sure is a problem.

There is one other vice common among the Amish men, but I don't see it as much a problem. Unexpected, to be sure, but that's the rest of the world's fault for equating Amish and angel. The next time you're to a horse sale and spot a crowd of fellows all huddled around, it could be they're discussing business. More than likely, though, somebody is in the process of telling what you might know of as an off-color story.

There was this boy and his name was Little Marvin. When Marvin was two, his dad died. A very sad affair. Around the time Marvin reached the age of five, he got to noticing that there were boys and there were girls in the world.

Marvin went to his mother and said, "Maw, how does the doctor tell the difference between a baby boy and a baby girl?"

Well, Marvin's mother is a sharp one and she said . . .

You know, there may be any number of women that are

reading this right now. This saga of Marvin, a real blue corker, doesn't need to go any further. Should any of you fellows happen by the sale barn sometime, though, be sure to look me up. You might find why this is an all-time favorite.

What I can tell you about is one of our Swartzentruber neighbors. You could tell they hadn't been married very long because they only had seven children, all boys. Things went pretty good one year so they decided to all go out to eat.

They went down to the Salt Fork Lodge, went in and got no more than sat down when the little one, Amos, said he had to go to the bathroom.

His mother asked if he could find it, he thought so and off he went. In a few minutes he was back.

"Well," Mom said, "did you find it?"

"No."

She sends the next oldest boy along with Amos to help, they come back and they didn't find it. She sends three, four, five and then six of them. Each time they come back, not having found it. Finally she sends all seven boys.

Well, the boys stay and stay and stay. Finally, after what seemed like an eternity, here they all come. Right over to the table and sit right down.

"Did you find it?" Mom asked.

"Finally," said the oldest one, Junior.

Mom said, "All right now, I saw other men get up, go out and then come back like they'd been to the restroom. They didn't seem to have any problem finding it. What was your problem?"

"No real problem, Mom," Junior said. "Amos just had his pants on backwards."

12

But then there is death

Assuming that I started thinking somewhat like an adult when I finished school at age fourteen, that's given me almost three decades of deliberate thought to get everything figured out. I think this is what causes depression because I haven't: not one single thing have I ever come to completely understand. As it stands right now, I'm still stuck on the very first issue I ever considered.

It still strikes me peculiar to this day that the people of Ohio, even with one hundred eighty years of practice, can't get used to the Amish. Ohioans aren't alone, though. Pennsylvania's had Deutschmen since 1730 and there's still all sorts of gawkers driving through Lancaster County. I can only imagine what those Amish who just moved into Oklahoma must be putting up with.

The Plain People aren't saints, mystic seers of another world or some secret society cloistered away from the world. Some of the best people on earth happen to be Amish, but

others happen to be Jewish—or Baptist or Catholic or whatever. Just like when that first farm of Amish Ohio was cleared
near Walnut Creek in 1809, the Plain People remain what
they've always been—just plain people.

From what I've read, there was another bunch of people
in Ohio long before the Amish. Nobody understood them,
either, nor did they try to from what I've seen. Instead these
different ones were lumped into one big category, even
though there were different factions of them, too. One faction
even called themselves Our People, just like us. With their
own language, dress and customs, they tried real hard to be a
people apart. Just like hanging a label on all of us as the
Amish, it was real easy to call them all the Indians.

Unlike the Native Americans, the Amish know exactly
what is happening to them. Land developers will take more
farmland this year, turning it into housing developments.
Tourists will keep coming, buying from foreign hucksters, and
never notice their car or bus break up another section of roadway. Self-appointed experts will continue to perpetuate mis-
information until all hope of understanding is gone. If we
continue to take and take and take from any resource, natural
or human, without ever giving back, we won't have much
worth saving before too long.

We know some Amish will cut their hair and go into the
world, never to return. Some claim one Amish in ten, just ten
percent, will be lost to the world and I've got no reason to
doubt that figure. More still will leave, going off to Amish Wisconsin or Amish Kentucky to be left alone if only for a few
more years. All because nobody much listens anymore, all too
happy living in bliss. After all, isn't that what ignorance is?

The loafers at the mill talk often of what Wisconsin must
be like. When asked if I'd consider moving to such a place, I
answer that I don't plan on it. I know all too well we cannot

figure what the next sunrise might bring, but for now we will
stay right here. Backwards by choice, we carry on until perhaps those of the world slow down enough to catch up to us.

I was thinking on that not long ago as I come walking in
from Levi's. They'd gone up to Wisconsin to see some family
and I was choring for them. It was about nine that morning,
maybe nine-thirty, the rain making down pretty good so that
you couldn't see the sun as I rounded the last bend to home.
Up the other way, trotting along in the buggy, here comes Old
Miller.

He stopped to visit a bit and we talked about that Wisconsin notion. Told him that story about the Swartzentrubers
going out to eat, too. Laugh, oh, you should of heard Miller
laugh at that one. He figured I should hop in the rig and go on
up to Bontrager's buggy shop and tell it again. Miller was
headed up there to get an old creeper wheel replaced.

Maybe I should have. Bontrager's always been real good
to me, ever since I sold the shop to him. It had been my
uncle's before, up until when he died of the home accident. It
was probably four years I ran the place, but pounding nails
was just more my cup of tea.

Bontrager and I used to talk about Uncle Lester a lot back
then, even today sometimes. What with all these modern
medicines, the doctors probably could of got his epilepsy
under control. Maybe he wouldn't of killed himself, maybe he
would. What with that and my folks deciding to leave the valley for good about the same time, I suppose the best thing
about that whole year is that it's over.

I remember shaking my head and figuring Sharon, the
lady of our house, was probably waiting for me. Maybe after
some breakfast and a little coffee I'd make my way up to visit
with the boys. With that we said our good-byes, the two of us
headed in a most opposite direction.

It's a funny feeling, one I could never describe, but I knew when I heard the siren a few minutes later exactly what had happened. I knew where they were headed. Some say the drunk never saw Miller's rig. Others claim Miller never felt a thing. The only thing for sure that morning was, in a heartbeat, Miller was dead.

We don't bear the drunk no grudge, that's not our way. Ours is not to pass judgment on the . . . well, I guess that's better left to the court system. Still, it gives you something to think about as you listen to a funeral being preached for four hours at the home place.

With luck Miller will find his paradise. Still, it gives you even more to think on when you've dug your friend's grave and then cover it over for eternity. For the want of a little breakfast, my friend, I would be beside you today.

There was more than enough to be thought on that day as the sun began its decline. It was an hour or so before dark when half a dozen of us had congregated down at the mill. It was crisp, but not winter-cold yet that year. As a matter of fact, with the exception of substituting my black felt for the summer straw hat, I think I was wearing the exact same clothes I was wearing the beginning of October.

The crowd that had collected there was the usual group of loafers, though we still prefer to think of ourselves as the trustees of the Peoli Valley. At any rate, we was all standing there, sipping on a little of the homemade root beer Levi likes to brew up when all of a sudden, running down the road, here comes Samuel. He was running so fast I was afraid the barn was on fire.

"No, no," he managed to gasp. "It's my wife. The little one's on the way!"

Those somber faces of the loafers started to turn to smiles as we watched Samuel dash to the telephone booth to call Mike, the local fellow who likes to drive for the Amish. Sure enough, in just a few minutes, here comes Mike in his old blue Chevy pickup. He and Samuel talk, Samuel jumps in and off they go, down Old 23 headed for County Hospital.

Such a joyous occasion as this long-expected addition to the community called for another round of the root beer. We wasn't but three or four sips into the mug when here comes Mike, racing up the road past us and right on up the North Road.

The loafers were still in hysterics when Mike came racing back, this time blowing the air horn and hollering out the window. He was going quick, powerful quick in fact, but not so fast that we couldn't see that Samuel was sitting there in the cab of that truck with a feed sack over his head. It was the best reminder we could of had as to life's basics.

First there is birth, but then there is death. Only through rebirth will we survive. For every one who goes, another will take his place. For one more day, life will go on, even in Amish country.